Alferian

Gwydion

Mac Lir

The Witch's Wand

Alferian Gwydion MacLir is the Druidical name of Dr. James Maertens, a master wandmaker, wizard, and writer. Handcrafting wooden wands for clients worldwide, Alferian has also written *Wandlore: The Art of Crafting the Ultimate Magical Tool*, the first book-length treatment of real magic wands.

Dr. MacLir is a Druid Companion of the Order of Bards, Ovates, and Druids (OBOD), the largest international British Druid order. He is a Freemason and student of the hidden mysteries of nature and the human spirit. Presently the doctor lives, writes books and articles, makes wands, and builds steampunk gizmos at his home, Bardwood Lodge, in the Lake District of Minneapolis, Minnesota. He abides in perfect harmony with his wife, his daughter, his familiar Minerva, and a large collection of extraordinary hats.

The Craft, Lore & Magick of
Wands & Staffs

The
Witch's
Wand

Alferian Gwydion MacLir

Llewellyn Publications
Woodbury, Minnesota

FIRST EDITION
First Printing, 2015

Book design by Rebecca Zins
Cover design by Lisa Novak
Cover illustration by John Kachik
Interior illustrations by Mickie Mueller

Llewellyn is a registered trademark of Llewellyn Worldwide, Ltd.

Library of Congress Cataloging-in-Publication Data
MacLir, Alferian Gwydion, 1960—
   The witch's wand: the craft, lore & magick of wands & staffs / Alferian
Gwydion MacLir.—FIRST EDITION.
      pages   cm—(The witch's tools series ; # 2)
"The lore, history, and symbolism of the wand; how to make your own for
different uses or occasions; and lots of wand spells and rituals are included
in this book"—Publisher's summary.
  Includes bibliographical references.
  ISBN 978-0-7387-4195-6
1. Magic wands. 2. Witchcraft. I. Title.
  BF1626.M335 2015
  133.4'3—dc23
                                                                      2015028817

Llewellyn Publications
A Division of Llewellyn Worldwide Ltd.
2143 Wooddale Drive
Woodbury, MN 55125-2989
www.llewellyn.com

Printed in the United States of America

contents

5: How to Make a Witch's Wand   119

Contents

introduction

this little book in your hands is intended as an exploration of one of the most intriguing of the witch's tools—the wand. Though one of the four elemental altar tools customary in today's traditional witchery, the wand does not get a lot of attention, and it should. Though I am not myself a witch, per se, I am a spell-caster and trained ovate, one of the Druid grades with many similarities to the traditional wise woman or cunning man found in almost every period and culture of European history. While kings wield swords and tanks and kill millions across the pages of Europe's past, the unobtrusive country or village witch has gone about her or his business as healer, diviner, midwife, adviser, attuned to nature's ways. The witch's wand is a symbol of life, as well as personal and cosmic will.

This book sets out to introduce the reader to wands from my point of view as a wandmaker. I've made magic wands for witches, sorcerers, Druids, and all sorts of magical folk. I always hope that my wands, as they have gone out in the world to serve their owners, contribute to the wonder and enchantment of our world, empowering their owner with the divine light of the sun and the moon.

The first chapter attempts to answer the question of what a wand is in terms of what it does, and in the more abstract terms of the philosophical elements, which are the basis of Western magic. I also discuss wands in terms of the colors of magic, which is another good system for classifying and thinking about Witchcraft and magery.

The second chapter looks briefly at how magic wands have figured into literature and myth—the only places most people ever get a glimpse of one being used. Twentieth-century films, books, and television shows have represented wands much as in the old myths and legends, and I discuss the misconceptions in some of the more famous representations of wands at work.

Chapter 3 delves into the power inherent in a magic wand as a symbol—or if you prefer, an astral reality, for on the astral plane of existence (the plane of the moon) symbols are real things themselves. Chapter 4 gets back down to earth by discussing wood and stones and their magical properties, their usefulness in making wands, and a bit about antlers and magical cores. Chapter 5 introduces some methods for making your own wand—a subject I have covered in a lot more detail in my book *Wandlore: The Art of Crafting the Ultimate Magical Tool* (Llewellyn, 2011). If you read this book and want more in-depth wand information, then that's the book for you.

Chapter 6 delves into how to use a wand through gestures and the creation of geometric figures, runes, and magical symbols. Following this, chapter 7 gives just a few examples of how a wand is used in specific spells. This isn't a spell book (there are plenty of those), but some examples will give you the idea of the many ways a wand can be employed in your Witchcraft, including in meditation. Chapters 8 and 9 show how special wands can be made and used in seasonal celebrations, sabbats, and ceremonies of life.

My intention in all of this is to inform, instruct, and inspire you to work with your wand if you are a witch, and to understand the witch's wand if you aren't.

Blessed be!

What Is a Wand?

When people ask me what I'm doing with all those sticks labeled and filed away in my garden shed, I tell them "I make magic wands," and they say "Cool—what do you do with a wand?" This book is my answer (though I usually just say "you do magic" and leave it at that). At bottom, a wand is a pointing stick. It points and power goes forth. A person holds it and possesses power, authority, awesomeness.

It is a stick used to point at things or tap on them, to gesture, and to express one's desires through physical attitude. It is associated with the will, one's self-assertion of desire, that movement from emotion or thought to action. The will is not just what you wish for; it is what you go after. In other words, it is active, not passive. One can daydream about finding treasure or the perfect mate for hours a day but not be exercising the will, much less performing magic.

A wand is directive, like the baton of a maestro leading an orchestra. It directs powers latent in ourselves and in the cosmos, potentialities for creation. Just as the maestro's baton causes a response in the musicians of an orchestra, so the witch's wand causes a response in the spirits of nature, those underlying intelligences and forces woven together to create the infinite music of causality. By tuning the vibrations of nature to her own will and intention, a witch makes something completely new in a way very similar to the way a musician tunes and manipulates the vibrations of string or reed to create sounds.

When used as an altar tool for ceremonial purposes the wand's movements are usually slow and majestic. The wand may trace symbols such as a pentagram or other geometric polyhedron, or its connecting points, or symbols of another sort such as Norse runes or Bardic ogham fews. A wand may be used to cast the circle in which sacred space is created and the practitioner removed from the ordinary state of temporal life.

Such wands may be adapted to very specific symbolism. Different wands may be designed for different ceremonies, and different parts of the ceremony.

Witchcraft ceremonies may be complex or simple enough to perform alone. Each witch usually has his or her own wand, but the coven or grove might have wands that are used for different occasions. For example, a wand might be designed to be used specifically at Samhuinn or Yule. We will discuss this more later, but for a moment think of the possibilities. A wand for use at Samhuinn to draw upon the particular magic of the season—the opening of the veils between worlds, communication with the ancestors or other spirits—could be fashioned of black ebony, carved with skulls and adorned with a pommel stone of smoky quartz or obsidian. A Yule wand might be made of holly and carved with holly leaves and mistletoe, with a red carnelian stone, or one of green jade. Pine or fir would be another good choice for Yule because the evergreens represent eternal life.

When a wand is used as a tool in spellcraft, it serves a more specific purpose. Its motions are more directive than in a seasonal observance, used toward some specific goal. A talisman or sachet is enchanted with the assistance of a wand to help focus the attention of the witch upon the object of intention. When a spell is simply cast (as distinct from placed in an object or vessel) the wand is used to point the direction of the energy being projected. In healing, a wand is used to touch the patient and to manipulate the energy system of the body.

Though traditionally the athame is used for banishing rituals and even casting circles, the wand may be used equally well. In fact, I believe the wand is more appropriate to banish mischievous entities or create sacred space, because it is the instrument of the magical will. If banishing is done to keep out such beings, a steel-bladed dagger will be most suitable, its "separating" power cutting you off from what is outside the circle. However, if the intention is to open the portals of the four directions to admit good spirits, then the wand may be more appropriate. In some covens and groves, a staff is used to draw the circle of work. A long staff is another kind of wand, one designed for this kind of "vertical" direction of the will—creating a link between sky and earth.

The wand is well-suited to active kinds of magic. For example, directing intention, charging magical objects, casting magical circles, defending against astral beings, or sending magical messages. These transmit power outward. When you are centering yourself, entering a trance, focusing your power inward to perform healing or some kind of inner work upon yourself, the wand is less appropriate. If it is used, it is simply held calmly. However, a stone or cauldron might be a better choice of magical tool for such work because its feminine energy is more conducive to containing power rather than planting it.

The Witch's Wand and the Elements

There are four traditional elemental tools on a witch's altar: the wand, cup, pantacle, and athame. The bell, book, and candle, besom, and other tools of Witchcraft are equally important, but the four elemental tools bear a special importance because these four philosophical elements are the basis for magic just as the seven tones of a musical scale are the basis for Western music.

The four elements are described through the picture stories of the four suits of the tarot's minor arcana—swords, pentacles (or coins), wands, and cups. They correspond to air, earth, fire, and water, respectively. The tarot suit of wands is often illustrated with a walking staff and is also called rods or staves (or clubs if you are playing bridge). Some tarot decks give other clues about wands by depicting them as arrows or spears; yet, one usually thinks of wands as small enough to fit on an altar and be carried in the hand.

There is a tradition that a wand should be measured to match the forearm and hand of the user, from fingertip to crook of the elbow. That is about the right size, but as always, intuition should be your guide when selecting a wand for yourself, or making one. As with broom, athame, or any other tool, there are infinite possibilities for shape, adornment, and use. But the wand is kept small because its main use is pointing—an extension of your hand and index finger.

In the tarot, the suit of wands represents the element of fire, and most witches think of their wand as such. A few, including author Scott Cunningham—whose opinion is nothing to shake a stick at—have attributed the wand to elemental air instead. There are logical arguments for each idea, but they result in very different meanings for the tool.

In alchemical terms, fire is the element of flame, light, and heat, but also vibration, life, passion, growth, and change. Its word is *action*. Elemental air, by contrast, is the mental part of existence. Its word is *thought* or *reason*. Wands are usually wood and so come from living trees. As such, they preserve some of the dryad spirit of the tree, and this active energy or personality aids the witch's own will on the trans-material planes. Daggers—or swords (spades, from Spanish *espada*) as in the tarot—may seem fiery because metal is forged in a furnace, but it is charcoal, or wood that is the ancient fuel for fire. Fire comes from wood, and this primordial association is the basis of the wand's elemental correspondence.

The cards of the tarot suit of wands can tell us a good deal about what a magic wand is for. They indicate matters on the spiritual level of being, the higher planes of existence, not just the thoughts in your conscious mind. Swords express something like words and language: the mental act of naming persons and objects to separate one thing from another. That is the meaning of the sword blade as a metaphor—sundering, cutting apart, dissecting. Wands, on the other hand, express the will and intention of a witch, not merely thinking and analyzing, but acting, making a practical application of knowledge and thought.

One's will employs reason and thought to execute actions; it is the hand that directs the blade, when that blade is one's intellect. Put another way, your wand is the tool used to aid in connection to your whole self through spiritual action. We use the word *passion* to describe that driving force of will that forms our intentions to act.

In a later chapter, we will see that all four of the elements are integrated in a witch's wand. It is a tool of elemental fire; yet, it also contains the other three elements in its symbolic construction.

If this elemental symbolism is too abstract, consider the more tangible connection between passion and fire. When active, angry, or aroused, we get hot. The colloquial expression that someone sexually attractive is "hot" is an expression of the elemental fact. Sexuality is one of the deep roots of will or its most basic animal expression. The wand's association with will is sometimes expressed in terms of the traditional male and female archetypes. The wand is phallic and the cup or chalice yonic; the wand is assertive, the cup receptive.

The use of this complementary system of two forces or qualities goes back to prehistory. We find it in the Vedas of India, among the oldest spiritual texts, and we find it in the Mediterranean world as well. The Egyptian ankh is interpreted as a symbol of the phallus penetrating the yoni. Sexual union, with its transcendent state of consciousness, may have

Wanderings: Air or Fire?

DEPENDING UPON THE tradition, the wand is associated with either Fire or Air. Those Wiccans/Witches who favor the Fire association point to the relationship between Fire and wood. There was also an ancient belief that Fire was latent within wood and could be drawn out through the rubbing of sticks. Wiccans/Witches who assign the element of Air to wood relate to the wand as a branch that once swayed in the wind and stretched up into the sky. The branch was also once a resting place for birds, creatures of the air.

—Raven Grimassi, *Encyclopedia of Wicca & Witchcraft*

been the first thing that required a symbol to indicate what was beyond words. Poets have been trying to put it in words ever since! But when applied to the magic wand, don't forget that this is a metaphor.

Wielding the assertive, willful power of the symbolic phallus is likened to the "active" attitudes of the male in copulation. This does not mean that the Feminine is completely non-active—far from it. The plow in the furrowed earth is used as such a metaphor, as is the prehistoric planter pushing seeds into the soil with a planting stick. It is worth considering whether the first ancestor of the magic wand was not in fact just such a planting stick. For planting seeds is used as a metaphor for planting ideas, casting the seed-thought filled with will, as a way of speaking about spellcasting.

Like all magic tools, the witch's wand is a symbol. One does not need to use a wand at all when casting spells; it isn't the wand that contains the magic. A pointed finger or sharp gaze can serve just as well to direct one's intention. The advantage to using a wand is that it makes the intention visible in a dramatic way. The mind and cosmos respond on a primordial level through symbols. At its deepest sense, the phallus expresses anything that enters into something else and delivers something that will grow and bear fruit (or offspring), metaphorically speaking.

We call male and female "opposites": That is really a mistake for they are actually complements, ever-joined together yet ever-different, two parts of one whole. I prefer yang and yin to masculine and feminine, terms borrowed from the Indian and Chinese spiritual traditions.

In Chinese the ideograms for these words mean sunlight and shade. Also, the sunlit side of a mountain and the shadowed side—expressing the unity of the whole, which these two complementary forces make.

It is easier to understand intuitively than intellectually. That's why we use symbols. The magical forces at work are no more literally "male" and "female" than the electrical plugs and receptacles we call by those metaphoric names. The matter is even more confused by the use of "male" and "female" for the two poles of a battery alongside plus and minus signs. Because of this shorthand, people have developed the idea that the feminine is "negative" and the masculine "positive." Those terms are highly misleading when we also associate "positive" with "good" and "negative" with "evil." Better to clear all those associations out of your mind.

Although shortly, I will explain the two ends of a wand in terms of polarity, it must not be supposed that one pole is better than the other, or that one pole is good and the other not. You would not consider Earth's North Pole good and South Pole bad, would you? Of course not. Positive and negative are terms adopted in Western physics to explain the flow of electrical current or magnetic force. Positive is the source; negative the destination. The terms have their uses in talking about electro-magnetism, but it is dangerous to confuse them when speaking of magical intentions, as we shall see, because the "source" part of the magical energy in a wand is considered its "feminine" end and the "flow," if you will, down the shaft and out the point is characterized as "masculine"—again on a quasi-phallic analogy. I find the sexual metaphor more trouble than it is worth, frankly!

In this book, I will be sticking with the interpretation of the wand and will as belonging to fire, and the athame and intellect to air. There is another correspondence for these two complementary forces, as noted in the piece from Lon Milo DuQuette. The masculine or yang force is associated with the sun and the feminine or yin force is associated with the moon—which in turn are used in the Great Rite of witches to show the union of these two luminaries with the altar tools standing in. Using an athame for the solar force associates it not with will or phallus, but with Intellect and words. The "penetration" (I prefer "planting") of the blade into the cup seems confused to me, implying that the Word or male intellect (which has long been thought "superior") fertilizes the female as a sort of inert nature. This is mixed up with centuries of Christian philosophizing and the justification of a

Wanderings: Athames and Wands

THE TRADITIONS OF Paganism associate the athame (dagger or sword) with fire and the phallus principal, and the wand with air and the intellect. Indeed, the dramatic climax of the overtly sexual Great Rite of the Witches celebrates the union of male and female, sun and moon, fire and water by penetrating a cup with the athame. All symbolism is ultimately arbitrary, of course, but in my mind there is a visceral disconnect here. The dagger is a weapon of injury that stabs, slices, cuts, and severs flesh. Naturally, such a weapon penetrates the flesh, but in my mind it is a poor phallic symbol. I cannot imagine the female preferring a cold sharp blade of dagger piercing the "cup" of her vagina rather than the rounded tip of a warmly oiled wand.

—Lon Milo DuQuette, *Homemade Magick*

social order of male dominance. Such ideas and their symbols may indeed have gotten into traditional Witchcraft at some point in the past, but they seem to me mistaken on a deep level. That is, mistaken from today's more feminist point of view (which has come to be shared by many Pagans).

Wands and the Colors of Magic

When I was introduced to magic long ago, it was through the categories of color. The first was green magic, that of the forests and trees. At our family lake cabin I would retreat to the woods and settle at the foot of the trees, surrounded by green sunlight and the living, growing power of the standing people. The second color of magic for me was brown—a field of magic people today tend to take for granted. It is the magic of animals. Humans have the ability to domesticate animals, to husband them, to establish relationships and communication with them. Talking to animals is derided by some people but I grew up reading Hugh Lofting's Doctor Dolittle books, so animals have always been "people" to me. Brown magic is the magic of familiars too.

Each field of magic is associated with a color. One finds this type of association in candle magic especially, but it permeates the practice of the magical arts and is thus important when designing a wand. The color of a wand, the stones or crystals used at point or pommel, and the color used in symbols carved upon it, all may gather particular energies and express the purposes that you set for it.

Color correspondences differ from one practitioner to another and may differ markedly across cultures. In the Western world colors are associated with the four elements and the seven planets of classical astrology. Other colors not named in Newton's seven-color spectrum are also used, and the associations with ideas, emotions, and purposes are usually self-evident to someone raised in a particular culture.

The Four Elements
Earth: Black or Green

Air: Yellow or Sky Blue

Fire: Red or Orange

Water: Dark Blue or Ultramarine

The Seven Planets
Sun: Orange or Gold

Moon: Blue, Silver, or White

Mercury: Yellow

Venus: Green

Mars: Red

Jupiter: Indigo

Saturn: Violet or Black

The logic behind these associations may not be clear if you are not familiar with alchemical logic. Red for Mars is fairly straightforward, but Indigo for Jupiter or Green for Venus make sense after you understand with what kinds of etheric power the colors are associated. Venus, for example, associated with love and attraction, corresponds to the color green because that is the color of vegetable life and growth and sexuality on an instinctive level. Venus is not only a goddess of love, she is a nature goddess too.

Taking the matter from the opposite direction, as it were, one can list the fields of magic corresponding to each color thus:

Red
The physicality of the body, blood, vigor, physical healing of disease, and so also physical protection, strong sexual urges, enthusiasm, charity or brotherly love, the giving of oneself. The root chakra.

Orange
Material wealth and strength, mental ego strength, pride, self-confidence, courage, security, flamboyance, attraction of abundance, prosperity, performance, drama, conjuring, entertainment, joy. Also, encouragement, adaptability, stimulation, and kindness. The belly chakra.

Gold
Between orange and yellow; solar energies, strength of character, wealth, leadership, beauty, vitality, life, and nobility of character.

Yellow
The mind and nervous system, thought, abstract ideas, logic, mathematics, learning, organizing ideas, theorizing, communicating. Also charm, charisma, persuasion, clairvoyance, clairaudience, and prescience. Divination, or the part of divination to do with logical and intuitive interpretation of symbols. The solar plexus chakra.

Green
Fertility, plants, herbs, trees, growth, creation, money (in the United States where money is green), good luck; also herbal medicine, potions and poultices, instinctive actions and feelings. The heart chakra.

Blue
Emotions, feelings, relationships, astral perception, intuition, dreams, meditation, emotional healing, mental health, tranquility, empathy, grieving. The throat chakra.

Indigo

Change, transformation, weather, flight, travel, astronomy, astrology, cosmology, star magic, love of wisdom (philosophy), wise kingship, right action. The brow chakra.

Violet

Cosmic consciousness and power, authority, intensity, passionate (suffering) love or hate, ambition, a sense of mission or destiny, ecstasy, epiphany, higher (esoteric) cosmology. The crown chakra.

Ultraviolet or "Colorless"

Pure power, extremes, universals, sacred geometries, mathemagics, mastery of death and resurrection; sudden, radical transformations or changes; transfiguration, understanding of the cosmos in terms of numbers.

Brown

Animals and fertility, fecundity, health and nurture, hunting, animal familiars, guides, or guardian totems. Transformation into animals; the home; one's house or farm, domestication of animals, husbandry, communication or empathy with animals.

Black

Magic of night, deep caves, ocean abysses, outer space, death. Domination, binding, revenge, deception, confinement, concealment, limitation, cursing, brooding teenagers, and the Faustian search for unlimited self-gratification. Black magic also covers necromancy (the darkness of the tomb), blood sacrifices (death again), monsters, and seduction (concealment). Contrary to popular belief, black magic is not necessarily malicious. Its techniques can be used in defense of innocence and justice, or homeopathically to combat negative energies or the malefic works of others. The occult (what is hidden).

White

Purification and the quest for the astral light; the clarity of divine vision, enlightenment, truth, blessing, altruism, self-regeneration, self-sacrifice. White contains all other colors and is not really a color itself (the same can be said of black). White and black can each be thought of as an absence.

Gray

Matters of mystery, lore, books, the past, ancestors, ghosts, what has been forgotten, finding balance between light and dark; matters to do with the underworld. Grieving, communicating with ancestors or the dead.

Pink

Admixture of white and red. Relationships between persons, love, peace, cooperation, social skills, compassion, empathy, kindness, gentleness, sweetness.

One can create a wand specifically to perform magic in any of these color fields, but any wand can be used for any type of magic. The advantage of having dedicated wands is to help you focus your attention on the purpose of a spell. Imagining and visualizing the color will draw upon that part of your nature that corresponds to the color. Visualize projecting light of the particular color from your wand tip. Even black light can be visualized (and I don't mean ultraviolet). Black magic is often visualized as black smoke.

Your wand can contain all or more than one of these colors to evoke particular effects. A wand half white and half black, for instance, calls upon the checkered pattern of life, filled with fortune and misfortune, life and death, love and hate—in short, all oppositions. A wand of green and brown, to take another combination, would join together animal and vegetable magical fields and be splendid for gardening, farming, and animal work of all kinds, including healing—a farmer's wand, or a veterinarian's.

For more on the colors of magic, see Bonewits, Cunningham, and Zell-Ravenheart in the bibliography.

Wands as Gifts

Wands should not be given as gifts unless the recipient participates in the selection or design process. Every witch's principal wand should be designed and made by herself or himself, if possible. On the other hand, if you aren't satisfied with your own work, it is certainly fine to purchase (or receive) a work of art that inspires you. There are times when wands are used as gifts in order to convey a special message at a magical level. In certain Native American rituals wands are sent to the chiefs of tribes to invite them to come to a ceremonial gathering. This is like the engraved invitations we use for weddings or graduation ceremonies—the art adds a magical power to compel attendance. An invitation wand becomes a physical correlative of the deepness of intent behind the invitation and the magical quality of the event to which the person is being invited. Such an invitation cannot be refused.

Similarly, you might present a person with a wand bearing a rose quartz reservoir as a powerful expression of love and peace, just as you might give a lover or friend a pink rose. You could give a red wand as a symbol of passionate love, protection, or physical healing—especially of physical wounds. In such cases, the wand is used in a way similar to a talisman. It should receive appropriate ornamentation and be chosen of a wood the energies of which correspond to its purpose.

When you give another person a wand you make a deep gesture and create a permanent bond between you and the recipient. Remember this if you are tempted to give a person a black wand for malefic purposes. Cursing someone establishes a permanent connection between you and them (unless they destroy the wand). Giving the gift of healing, love, and good fortune also establishes a bond, and this can be just as bad as a curse if it ends up that the recipient becomes a constant drain on one's energies.

You may also make a specially colored wand for your own use: a red wand for healing work, a yellow wand for divinatory work, a green wand for green magic of life and growth, an indigo wand for magical quests for wisdom and knowledge.

One can find wood of many colors especially among exotics such as bloodwood (red), ebony (black or brown), mahogany (brown), purpleheart for violet, yellowheart for yellow. Paint or stain of a light-colored wood can also give color, though not quite as deeply.

Keep It Secret, Keep It Safe!

"What do I do with my wand when I'm not using it?" asks the novice. A wand may be displayed openly nowadays within the privacy of your home or shrine, and there are many places where no one will trouble about it. That is a matter for you to decide about your community or family. However, it is better

Wanderings: Many Wands

WANDS CAN BE commercially bought, or disguised as everyday tools. I've known witches who use their wooden kitchen spoon and mechanics who use their screwdriver... In ritual, wands are used to cast the boundary of a circle, and to direct energy in general. I use wands for healing, and have several different wands depending on the situation. You can have more than one wand. Most witches have at least two. One of the two is the internal wand.

—Christopher Penczak, *The Outer Temple of Witchcraft*

to keep your wand wrapped in silk and inside a sturdy box when it is not in use. This will keep it from getting dusty and from being too much exposed to daily life. You want your wand to be special, sacred, and reserved for magical use.

You alone should handle your wand. It may do no harm for someone else to handle it, but you may not know until it is too late. You do not want others transferring their energies into your wand.

The dryad spirit within a wood wand is a living creature, and each wand has its own personality. So it is best not to leave your wand too long in its box. Give it your attention and energy regularly if possible, and put it to magical use as often as you can. If a wand is dedicated to a specific sabbat or purpose, it may only be used at long intervals. That does not mean you should not take it out in between times to recharge it with your etheric power and the power of the universe through simple solar or lunar rituals.

Once you have a wand, it will become part of you. The branch or stones that call to you to become your wand know you, perhaps better than you do yourself. Trees and stones can see into the astral and spiritual dimensions much more easily than we poor ego-hampered and short-lived primates. The dryad spirit of the tree will join with you in achieving your intentions and making them manifest in the world of matter and forms.

Wanderings: Dryads

SOMETIMES LYING ON the hillside with the eyes of the body shut as in sleep...I saw fountains as of luminous mist jetting from some hidden heart of power, and shining folk who passed into those fountains inhaled them and drew life from the magical air. They were, I believe, those who in the ancient world gave birth to legends of nymph and dryad. Their perfectness was like the perfectness of a flower...More beautiful than we, they yet seemed less than human, and I surmised I had more thoughts in a moment than they through many of their days. Sometimes I wondered had they individualised life at all, for they moved as if in some orchestration of their being. If one looked up, all looked up. If one moved to breathe the magical airs from the fountains, many bent in rhythm. I wondered were their thoughts all another's, one who lived within them, guardian or oversoul to their tribe?

—AE (George William Russell) from "The Many-Colored Land" in *The Candle of Vision*

This dryad is the secret of the tree and the secret of the magic wand. For it is a transcendent spirit who lives long and lives a life of utter interconnection. The dryad, or consciousness of a tree, is in the tree's physical body and extends beyond it, interlaced with surrounding trees, in competition with them, in cooperation and sympathy with other members of the plant and animal kingdoms. Insects may live within its branches and roots; they may eat it away and kill it; animals may live there and reproduce, may feed upon its fruits and buds.

Likewise, human souls depend upon the tree for oxygen and it draws carbon dioxide from our breath to sustain its life. It absorbs the light of the sun to make its food, which is the basis of all food. The trees sacrifice themselves for human will in the making of shelter or fuel for fire. The "thinking" of dryads, if one can use the term, is slower than ours and non-verbal but far more deliberate. J. R. R. Tolkien captured this quality when he created the Ents of his fictional Middle Earth in *The Lord of the Rings*—the tree shepherds with their day-long conversations and slow deliberation.

Dryads are creatures who know about growth and transformation, who have the patience to carry creative work out for as long as it takes. They also have no trouble enduring the inconvenience of animals feeding upon their nuts, nesting in their branches, and even wrecking their tissues with tunneling larvae. It is part of life. In other words, dryads do not have such a human concept as "good" and "evil" in the abstract. Competition for light and nutrients is part of their will, but they do not waste time worrying about those things they cannot control, such as drought, flood, fire, and disease.

When you create a wand with a dryad spirit from a particular tree, you join with that spirit and with all the qualities of that tree to enhance your own powers and become something far larger than yourself. As in any magical relationship to non-human entities, it is wise to keep the matter secret and sacred so that it cannot be profaned by the disbelief, fear, or laughter of others.

The possession of a wand made carefully with the consciousness of the dryad of the tree awake and present will create the opportunity to see existence from a much broader perspective. In addition, the tree spirit will lend its power and magical propensities to your own will when you call upon its aid.

The Greeks considered dryads to be deities, albeit "minor" ones. This does not mean that they are not powerful; indeed calling upon their aid may be more effective than calling upon "major" deities such as Zeus and Diana, or whatever names you may use. These major deities are vast and general powers of the sky, the moon, etc. Calling upon a local spirit, such as that of a tree or stone, may permit much more focused work. Your own will can more easily get the attention of a minor deity, especially when it becomes more familiar as the spirit of your wand. In sum, this is a good way to think of your wand—as if you are carrying a deity in your hand.

Now that we have discussed what a magic wand is, and the vast range of activities for which it can be used, let's turn to the historical view of the witch's wand—where did wands come from, and how are they represented in myth and story?

Wands in Legend and History

Prehistory and the Ancient World

The whole business of magic wands might, arguably, be traced back to the Greek god Hermes and his caduceus, which he carries as herald of the gods and also uses for casting magic spells. Scholars of prehistoric cultures must rely on artifacts and pictures, and upon the myths and legends that were recorded in place of that more factual and limited discourse we call "history" today. Prof. Goblet d'Alviella, in his book *The Migration of Symbols,* says:

> The Caduceus is one of the symbolic figures which have tried in the highest degree the patience of scholars. Its classic appearance of a winged rod, round which two serpents are symmetrically entwined, is very far removed from its

primitive form. Greek monuments make known to us a period when it consisted of a circle, or a disk, placed on the top of a stick, and surmounted by a crescent, making thus a kind of figure 8 open at the top [thus:][1]

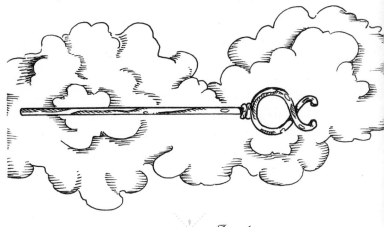

A caduceus

---

1   *The Migration of Symbols* by Count Goblet d'Alviella (1894).
The author of this seminal work on the migration of symbols from one culture to another was a nineteenth-century Belgian lawyer and Masonic scholar.

This primitive form can be interpreted in many ways. The rod resembles the phallus and the circle the vagina or womb, and the "horns," the ovaries. Alternatively, the line and the circle are the two most fundamental geometric shapes after the point. From these all other geometries are constructed, and this is the basis of magic—in number and form.

The Hermes glyph appears so often on Phoenician monuments that no one can tell whether the caduceus was borrowed by the Phoenicians from Greece and Hermes, or whether the Greeks derived it from the Phoenicians. Similar symbols were used in Libya and Carthage (a city founded by the Phoenicians of Tyre). There it seems to be a solar symbol for the dying and reborn son of the God and Goddess, which expresses the cycle of day and night. This is appropriate for a wand, for the sun is also acknowledged by many religions to be the source and symbol of divine will and creation.

According to Homer, the caduceus is a rod of gold that alternately "charms the eyes of men and calls them from their slumbers" (Homer, *Odyssey*, Book V: lines 47, 48). It leads the dead to Hades and can bring them back to the light of day, and it changes all it touches into gold. Gold is the metal of the sun and is also a symbol of purification and perfection, which is the ultimate goal of all magic. The Roman philosopher Epictetus, demonstrating that all things considered evil may also be interpreted as good, says of his method:

A winged globe staff

This is the magic wand of Hermes. "Touch what you will," he says, "and it will turn to gold." Nay, bring what you will and I will turn it to good. Bring illness, bring death, bring poverty, bring reviling, bring the utmost peril of the law-court: the wand of Hermes will turn them all to good purpose! (Matheson, *Discourses*)

Today we still find this idea in the colloquial phrase "it's golden" to refer to something that is perfect and good.

Before the Greek culture rose to its heights, Mesopotamia was the center of human civilization. There, a pair of horns were used to represent divine power and a sphere with horns (or the two horns of the crescent moon) depicted the head of a priest, mage, or witch, drawing upon what is above to affect what is below. A winged globe on a staff is another style of this eldest of magic wands—wings also signifying communication with the celestial realms.

This winged globe is found in ancient Egyptian images and in symbols representing Baal Hamman, male consort of the Goddess Astarte in Phoenicia. Baal, like Hermes, was an initiator and messenger of higher powers—as Goblet d'Alviella puts it, "an intermediate agent between mankind, and the superior divinity" (*Migration of Symbols*, note 2, 229).

The construction of the rod tipped with the circle and crescent (or winged sphere) derives from the older image of the sacred tree. With the addition of the two intertwining serpents, the symbolism is complete. Serpents are life force,

Wanderings: Mercury's Magic Wand

IN ORDER THAT he might perform his duties as messenger more swiftly, Mercury was given by Jupiter wings for his feet, and a winged cap for his head. He is said to have invented the lyre, or harp, and to have given it to the Sun-god Apollo, who gave him in return a magic wand called Caduceus, which had the power of making enemies become friends. Mercury, in order to test its power, put it between two fighting snakes, and they at once wound themselves round it. Mercury ordered them to stay on the wand, and, in statues and pictures, the god is nearly always holding in his hand this wand with the snakes twisted round it.

—Reginald C. Couzens, *The Stories of Months and Days*

immortality, joined together in the act of regeneration. The wand itself is the World Tree, the Tree of Knowledge, the Tree of Life.

From Chaldea to Phoenicia to Egypt and westward, the sacred tree is shown with two animals or two human forms on either side. They flank the stem and regard the fruit of the branches at the top of the tree. In the caduceus, the foliage becomes wings and the two flanking creatures intertwined snakes. The intertwining is serpentine mating—that is, harmony or the joining of yin and yang. This helix shape formed by the snakes resembles DNA and the kundalini channels of energy up and down the spine found in yogic teachings. The wand alludes to the spine and its movement of energies inward and outward from the user.

While Hermes's caduceus is one root of the magic wand in Western culture, it is not the only wand to be found in the Greek myths. In Homer's *Odyssey*, the hero's encounter with the goddess Circe reveals a powerful magical woman. Circe is described as appearing "with broidered robe and magic wand" (Flaccus, *Argonautica*) and has many potions with which she performs her magic. She also has prescient dreams—not surprising for the daughter of Helios, Titan of the sun, and the nymph Perseis. One can see this lineage in the caduceus wand: Helios being the circle or sphere, the sun's disc, the horns of the moon (or curve of the cup) the water nymph, and the downward extending shaft the magic manifested like a ray of light to be wielded by Circe. One of the most fundamental images you should keep in your mind when using a magic wand is that you are holding a ray of light.

To Homer, Circe may have been malicious, but interpreted through more modern eyes, she is a sexually assertive woman (a frequent characteristic of goddesses). Like the Sirens, whom Odysseus also encounters, Circe's beauty, power, and voice subdue the Hero and reverse the polarities of the archetypal Masculine and Feminine, rendering him passive; that is, the object of passion, feeling, will. Put another way, the phallus-wielding woman controls the assertive, often violent energies of the Masculine as it is found in men. A male witch wielding the symbolic phallus of the wand channels his own assertiveness and violent tendencies into constructive will.

To the modern mind, tutored by depth psychology, there is nothing wrong with such a reversal. Indeed, it is healthy and necessary. Night becomes dominant, day becomes dominant, each in turn. Circe uses her wand to turn Odysseus's crew into pigs, partly as a commentary on their animal nature, and partly to isolate Odysseus as the object of her desire. Granted, turning people into pigs does not seem constructive. Yet, in so many of these animal transformation stories we find that living as an animal and then being changed back into a human gives a person a completely new understanding of life. One might even think of it as a shamanic journey in animal form.

Nevertheless, once outfoxed by Odysseus (with the help of a sprig of an herb given him by Hermes), Circe changed the men back with a magic ointment and then helped Odysseus by telling him of the dangers he would encounter as he continued his long voyage home. Taking in the whole story, Circe is more helpful than harmful and while we are not given her initial motives, one suspects that she turned intruders into animals for her own protection. Circe was wise in the ways of herbs, and the use of the wand in this case seems to be to activate the power already ingested in the form of a "drug."

Another ancient influence on our ideas of magic wands and their uses comes from the Bible. This collection of hundreds of years of Hebrew myths, legends, and chronicles draws upon Babylonian stories and material from Egypt (both places the ancient Hebrews were held captive as slaves). In the story of the Hebrew prophet Moses, who confronted the Pharaoh of Egypt to free the Hebrew slaves, a rod of magic is employed. It is actually the rod of Aaron, who was the brother of Moses and the ancestor of the Hebrew temple priesthood. The rod is used to strike a stone and make water spring forth from it. It is also turned into a serpent in a competition with Pharaoh's magicians. The Egyptian priests throw down their rods

Wanderings: Circe and the Men of Ulysses

THEY ARRIVED AT the Æaean isle, where Circe dwelt, the daughter of the sun. Landing here, Ulysses climbed a hill, and gazing round saw no signs of habitation except in one spot at the centre of the island, where he perceived a palace embowered with trees. He sent forward one-half of his crew, under the command of Eurylochus, to see what prospect of hospitality they might find.

As they approached the palace, they found themselves surrounded by lions, tigers, and wolves, not fierce, but tamed by Circe's art, for she was a powerful magician. All these animals had once been men, but had been changed by Circe's enchantments into the forms of beasts. The sounds of soft music were heard from within, and a sweet female voice singing. Eurylochus called aloud and the goddess came forth and invited them in; they all gladly entered except Eurylochus, who suspected danger.

The goddess conducted her guests to a seat, and had them served with wine and other delicacies. When they had feasted heartily, she touched them one by one with her wand, and they became immediately changed into swine, in "head, body, voice, and bristles," yet with their intellects as before. She shut them in her sties and supplied them with acorns and such other things as swine love.

—*Odyssey* of Homer as adapted in *Bulfinch's Mythology: The Age of Fable* by Thomas Bulfinch and they turn into snakes. Moses commands Aaron to throw down his rod and it also turns into a snake, which then proceeds to eat all the other snakes. Usually, in art, these rods are staves, and Aaron's rod in particular is used as a walking staff. Of course, as is so often the case, the person telling the story calls the good guys' magic a "miracle" performed by God, while the bad guys' magic is "just magic." It is part of the purpose of such myths to prove whose gods are stronger.

Moses supposedly raised his staff to part the Red Sea so the Hebrews could cross over and escape Egypt. It is a good example of how the staff may serve as a symbol of the mage's intention, and the drawing down of power from heaven.

I myself think of drawing on the power of heaven in its literal meaning—the sky. The "heavens" refer to the stars and it is from the constellations and planets that the powers of causality act upon the earth plane of existence. The ancient Babylonians (or Chaldeans) were great astrologers, and their understanding of the influence of planetary and stellar configurations is one of the foundations of Western magic.

Egypt, too, bears witness to the divine power of a wand, which in the following example resembles a key.

The Great Mother wields a magic wand which the ancient Egyptian scribes called the "Great Magician." It was endowed with the two-fold powers of life-giving and opening, which from the beginning were intimately associated the one with the other from the analogy of the act of birth, which was both an opening and a giving of life. Hence the "magic wand" was a key or "opener of the ways," wherewith; at the ceremonies of resurrection, the mouth was opened for speech and the taking of food, as well as for the passage of the breath of life, the eyes were opened for sight, and the ears for hearing. Both the physical act of opening (the "key" aspect) as well as the vital aspect of life-giving (which we may call the "uterine" aspect) were implied in this symbolism. (Smith, "Artemis")

Celtic Legend and Myth

In the principal Welsh (Cymric) cycle of myths, the Mabinogi (or Mabinogion), there are several instances of wand use that can give us a sense of technique and method. Perhaps the greatest mage in Cymric legend is Math, son of Mathonwy. Lady Charlotte Guest, one of the most well-known translators of the tales says,

> The mystical arts of Math appear to have descended to him from his father, whose magic wand is celebrated by Taliesin, in the *Kerdd Daronwy*. It is there asserted that when this wand grows in the wood, more luxuriant fruit will be seen on the banks of the Spectre waters. (Guest, *The Mabinogion*, note 413a)

The statement is poetic and a little cryptic but may be interpreted to mean that such wands as Math's grow upon the trees of the forests and the presence of the power in such trees will be known because they are near Faerie ("spectre") springs or lakes upon the banks of which will be found especially luxuriant fruit. This may also allude to the Hazels of Wisdom, which grew on the banks of such a spring. Their abundant hazelnuts fell into the waters and were eaten by a great salmon who lived in the pool. Thus this salmon became the Salmon of Wisdom, holding within all the knowledge and understanding of the cosmos. The hazel tree is one that is often used for magic wands.

Math has a mage nephew named Gwydion, who is as much of a trickster as Hermes. Because of the tricks he played upon his uncle and king, he and his brother Gilvaethwy are turned into deer by the magic wand of Math. After living a year as deer, they are turned into swine, then into wolves for their punishment. The three years also result in the brothers producing offspring—fawn, piglet, and wolf cub—each of which Math turns, with his wand, into boys, whom he names and adopts as faithful warriors as a way of recompensing himself for the many warriors lost in the war Gwydion started as part of his trickery.

Math's wand, in this story serves as an instrument of transformation and justice. It projects the will of Math and compels the will of Gwydion and that of his brother into channels they cannot control. That is, the trickster-thief and the rapist, respectively, are turned to animals to reflect their beastly nature and are forced into copulation with each other in this form, thus reversing the polarities of their masculinity. There is a lot of implied phallicism in this story. The bad uses of the male self-assertion (that is, selfishness), that leads to harm is countered by the good phallic power of the just king—sort of.

Another part of this story centers on the maiden who is employed by Math to hold his feet in her lap whenever he is on his throne ruling his kingdom. This deal is a requirement, not a luxury. The maiden he was employing for this purpose is raped by Gilvaethwy and so Math recompenses her by marrying her himself, thus making her queen. Yet, he needs a new lap-maiden for his footstool. Rather foolishly, one must think, he asks Gwydion to recommend someone. He recommends his sister Arianrhod, who is supposed to be a maiden. Math tests her virginity by setting his wand on the floor and making her step over it. When she does, she spontaneously gives birth to two sons. It's a complicated story, but the long and short of it is that Arianrhod flees in shame and embarrassment, Math confiscates the older of the two offspring and names him Dylan (thus acquiring another young godling of his own), while Gwydion secretly grabs the second offspring, who is a mere fetus. Gwydion uses his magic to gestate the boy in a wooden chest and then takes him for his own son. Weird goings-on at the court of Math.

The interpretation of these bardic tales requires a symbolic reading and I won't attempt it fully here. Suffice to observe that Math's magic wand again acts in the role of phallus, bringing about miraculous births and revealing truth. As before, the offspring of the magic are themselves magical. There are other stories about Arianrhod, whose name means "silver wheel," indicating that she is a moon goddess. If taken so, then the magic that occurs, while represented in the story as a trick upon a woman who has had illicit sex (or more to the point, has lied on her job application), is actually the act of fertility and creation itself, which the phallus symbolizes. In other words, the wand and the Lunar cup are brought together in that most primordial act of magic, the creation of new life. In another case, Math employs his wand to make a wife for Llew Llaw Gyffes out of flowers.

In Irish myths and legends we find the Druidic wand (*slat an draoichta*, "rod of magic") used for transformation into animals too. There are several stories in which characters are punished by being turned into hounds, swans, pigs, and hawks. In one case, the mage changes his brothers into hounds to smell out which in a group of pigs is actually a man who has changed himself into a swine to hide. In another, a Druid wand was used to cause a king to break out in boils and ulcers, eventually going mad. In yet another tale, information about a foe is sought by means of a Druidical fire kindled with

Wanderings: Druid Wands

MANANNAN OF THE Tuatha De Danann, as a god-messenger from the invisible realm bearing the apple-branch of silver, is in externals, though not in other ways, like Hermes, the god-messenger from the realm of the gods bearing his wand of two intertwined serpents. In modern fairy-lore this divine branch or wand is the magic wand of fairies; or where messengers like old men guide mortals to an underworld it is a staff or cane with which they strike the rock hiding the secret entrance.

The Irish Druids made their wands of divination from the yew-tree; and, like the ancient priests of Egypt, Greece, and Rome, are believed to have controlled spirits, fairies, daemons, elementals, and ghosts while making such divinations.

—W. Y. Evans-Wentz, *The Fairy-Faith in Celtic Countries*

rowan wood. In this case no wand is employed, but we gain insight into the magical qualities of rowan wood in spells of information.

Although "Druid wands" are mentioned in a number of stories about these Celtic wizards, most of the magic performed by Druids is not represented as requiring a wand. It is a little hard to judge whether the wand is not mentioned because it is assumed, or because, as we find elsewhere, magic may be performed simply with the hands and will. Witches today know this to be the case, especially where broad effects are created. The projection of intention is effected through words, gestures, and symbols—a wand is a symbol used for gesturing.

India and the Far East

In Eastern lands we find that magic wands are often staves like walking or hiking sticks. In recounting the ceremony of a yogi's initiation on page 82 of his book *Occult Science in India* (1919), Louis Jacoilliot writes:

> The chief Guru who presides at the ceremony, hands him [the initiate] a bamboo stick containing seven joints, some lotus flowers, and powdered sandal-wood, and whispers in his ear certain mentrams [mantras] of evocation, which are only made known to persons in his condition. This stick is not intended to help support his steps or to be of any

assistance to him in walking. It is the magic wand used in divination and all the occult phenomena.

In Chinese Taoist legends we also find wands used by sages for transforming objects, for controlling magical beings, and for defending against or breaking magical weapons, such as swords.

> To conquer T'ung-t'ien Chiao-chu was more difficult, but after a long fight Chun T'i waved his Wand of the Seven Treasures and broke his adversary's sword. The latter, disarmed and vanquished, disappeared in a cloud of dust. Chun T'i did not trouble to pursue him. The battle was won. (Werner, *Myths and Legends of China*, 321)

The Middle Ages

After the fall of Rome and the fragmentation of its empire, the Greco-Roman world of scholarship and literature fell apart. We have only a few clues about the practice of Witchcraft as such, but a fair amount about sorcery of a more academic nature. In these, wands play a role. Some books were preserved by the Arabs, including magical lore, because medical and scientific lore was not distinguished from much of what we would call "magic" today. In fact, this distinction between licit medicine and illicit magic mainly emerges in the Middle Ages, with the rise to authority of Christian bishops and the Roman Catholic Church.

Magic, while it was officially condemned, was still practiced, as we learn from the medieval grimoires and the books of natural philosophy, such as those of Agrippa. The idea that plants, animals, and stones had innate "virtues" was taken as a fact and not really considered to be "magic" as such. The church was more worried about the sort of magic that involved calling up demons to be one's personal servants. We see this a lot in the grimoires, which in all probability were written by Christian monks, since they were practically the only people who knew how to read and write back then.

One of the most famous of these books is *The Greater Key of Solomon*, which at its beginning describes the making of magical tools. Among these tools are swords and daggers—useful in threatening astral baddies into submission. However, a wand and a staff are also described as among the tools.

The staff should be of elderwood, or cane, or rosewood; and the wand of hazel or nut tree, in all cases the wood being virgin, that is of one year's growth only. They should each be cut from the tree at a single stroke, on the day of Mercury, at sunrise. The characters shown should be written or engraved thereon in the day and hour of Mercury.

As can be seen in the illustrations, the "staff" is no larger than the "wand." The only difference is that the wand is tapered to a point. The staff is for holding up vertically, the wand for pointing at things. There is emphasis placed upon

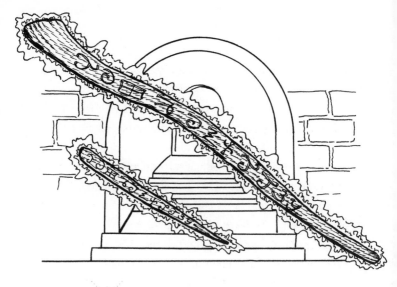

A solomonic staff and wand

the wood used and the idea of it being "virgin." This latter stipulation is one that I have long found suspect—or at least confusing. I should say that the "virginity" of the wood means that it is a branch that has never been used for anything else. You may wish to spend some time "courting" the tree and the branch, but a branch only one year old is not much of a branch in most cases—more of a twig. And knowing that a branch is only one year away from budding would require a great deal of observation and foresight! Sometimes writers of magical instructions slip in confusing bits for the unwary, to make following them impossible. It might also be a scribal error or mistranslation. In any case, the important thing is to find a branch of the right size, not any specific age.

While hazel is an excellent wand wood, cane might be a bit fragile. (Still, there is the bamboo staff of the Hindus…) Rosewood is splendid, but apart from rose symbolism, I am not sure why it should be picked out especially. Elder is a viable choice but will yield a hollow wand because of its pithy core. More understandable and also traditional from some grimoires is almond wood. Almond is a fine choice because of its fruitfulness and nurturing qualities, providing us with food, and because it is a close-grained and smooth wood adaptable for the carving of letters and symbols.

The figures in the *Key of Solomon* show that particular symbols or letters must be carved or written on the wand, and this is an ancient practice among mages: The use of the written word or special marks to convey intention and drawing on divine power. The text goes on to give a simple prayer as the enchantment for the wand and staff in the medieval Judeo-Christian context:

> *ADONAI, Most Holy, deign to bless and to*
> *consecrate this Wand, and this Staff, that*
> *they may obtain the necessary virtue, through*
> *Thee, O Most Holy ADONAI, Whose kingdom*
> *endureth unto the Ages of the Ages. Amen.*

The two instruments are then "perfumed and consecrated" in some way not explained—though probably with scented oil or incense and water or fire for the consecration. Then one is to "put them aside in a pure and clean place for use when required." Elsewhere the text mentions wrapping all instruments in silk.

While these ideas come from Judeo-Christian ceremonial magic of the Middle Ages, the prayer may be adapted to the "Lord" (the meaning of "Adonai") in Witchcraft just as well. I offer a fuller consecration and dedication ceremony later on in this book. The key to the ceremonial blessing or consecration is to "make sacred," and this must be done according to your own beliefs. However different from Witchcraft the clerical magic of the medieval monks was, some principles are similar.

Fairytale Wands and Modern Fantasy

We find witches with wands in the "fairytales" of Andrew Lang, such as one instance from *The Grey Fairy Book* (1900) where a princess escapes from the castle in which she has been held prisoner with the help of her nurse, who is actually a witch. The nurse enchants a wheelbarrow and a bear skin to act as magical transportation and magical disguise respectively. The princess uses the bear skin to good effect, playing tricks on a prince and (using the magic wand) turning the bear skin into a ball gown made of moonbeams. ("The Bear" from Lang, *Grey Fairy Book*.) In "The Frog" a helpful frog is transformed into a lovely woman by means of a witch's wand (Lang, *The Violet Fairy Book*).

Likewise in traditional tales from Scotland and England we find witches and fairies with wands, which they sometimes lend to the hero or heroine of the story. Such wands can turn people into stones or kill monsters, such as the Red Ettin, a giant with three heads whose tale is rather reminiscent of "Jack the Giant Killer." (Jacobs, *English Fairy Tales*). In another tale called "Kate Cracknuts" the heroine steals a fairy wand from a fairy baby and uses it to cure her sister of a magical illness (Jacobs, *English Fairy Tales*).

Disney movies popularized the fairy godmother with a wand, especially in *Sleeping Beauty* where there are a host of different-colored fairy godmothers, each with her own wand.

In *Cinderella*, the heroine's fairy godmother transforms a pumpkin into a coach and mice into footmen with her wand. This is where we get the idea of the wand with a star on the top, held more like a scepter than a pointer, and the star directed toward the object of intent. It is not a bad idea, really, if one considers the star symbolic of the powers of the heavens. Astrology and the stars are often considered the source of magical power.

In these cases, as in most fictional representations of wand use, the mage can do anything, and transformations are especially emphasized. In the case of *Sleeping Beauty*, the fairies offer blessings to the baby, except for the last one who is bad and gives her the curse that will lead to her magical sleep.

Tinkerbell, the fairy in *Peter Pan*, is given a wand by Disney. Generally, representations of fairies in folklore do not describe them using wands. They perform their magical appearances and disappearances without even doing spells, so far as the observer can tell. In *The Fairy-Faith in Celtic Countries*, Evans-Wentz collected stories from locals in Ireland and other parts of the Celtic-speaking world. He recorded many stories of what we might call curses and bewilderment charms, but in no case do the Fair Folk need wands or even words to create their effects. It might be worth noting, however, that the tales do not usually report seeing fairies do anything. The magic just happens to the poor mortal who annoys those Good People.

Of course, the place in modern fantasy novels where one encounters magic wands most prominently is in the Harry Potter stories of J. K. Rowling. In her work, wands are at the center of magic and young wizards and witches cannot control their powers without a wand. As in most fantasy stories, magic is largely a matter of transforming things or knocking people about. There are lock-opening spells, light-making spells, and so forth, but what occurs most often in these stories is using a wand for offense, defense, or just making pretty things. Levitating objects, spells to do the dishes, enchanted clocks, and so forth are mentioned, but no real insight is given into how magic actually works.

Rowling's representation of how wands are made is nevertheless interesting. She made the magic of wands of the Potterverse dependent upon two things. First, that they come from a special kind of wand tree inhabited by magical creatures called bowtruckles. (Fay folk by any other name...) Second, a core made out of the bodily ephemera of a magical creature has to be included in the wand. Rowling does not describe how this is done, but everyone in her stories had to have a wand core of unicorn hair, phoenix feather, dragon heartstrings, or something for it to work. Some creature who possesses magic "naturally," so to speak, adds that power to the wood from a tree. Bowtruckles are rather reminiscent of dryads, but they are not described as being the spirit of the trees.

Nor does Rowling's wandmaker, Mr. Ollivander, explain the reasons for using different kinds of wood. It is implied that different people's personalities have an affinity with different kinds of trees. Harry Potter's wand is Holly, a wood with fiery and kingly connotations and linked to eternal life, which does have a bearing on Harry's story. Lord Voldemort, the baddie in the Harry Potter books who is trying to make himself immortal by magical means, has a wand of yew wood. Yew is a tree associated with churchyards and the journey of the dead. Its evergreen nature links it to the cycle of death and rebirth. Which is appropriate for Voldemort, though yews are not evil or sinister in reality.

The idea of a magical core is one I have adopted in my own wandmaking. Magical creatures such as unicorns and phoenixes are inhabitants of the astral plane, the dreamworld. Their bodily ephemera are therefore to be found in that plane of existence and may be enchanted into the wand by means of the magical imagination. The value of this method is that the wand of wood, with a stone pommel reservoir or crystal point and an animal core, incorporates the three kingdoms of animal, vegetable, and mineral.

Symbolizing the "kingdoms" of living things is powerful in the same way as symbolizing the four elements. These are imaginal powers upon which we organize the cosmos for magical purposes. The more a witch's wand can be tied to these great categories of nature, the more sacred it becomes.

So, the tellers of tales often give us good clues about magic wands and they often lead us astray with the devices of story-telling. For the most part, stories of magic, in Western culture at least, tend to oversimplify magic, making it seem simple and straightforward for those witches who are born with a special power. Sometimes they represent sages, such as Merlin of the Arthurian tales, who seem to have studied an art, but even in Merlin's case it is implied that he was born to it. Wands are sometimes represented as carrying the power in themselves, but more often are the transmitters of power possessed by the witch herself. Is it "real" or not? The question of reality is not as simple as people today like to imagine, and so, let us turn to the matter of symbols and their reality.

The Wand as a Symbol

The medium for manifesting intention is the symbol. Symbols such as runes, sigils, and witch's signs are all well-known and understood to convey power and meaning. A witch's tools do the same. The "mechanism" of a wand, if you will, is symbolism.

The wand, speaking geometrically, is a line or arrow. A line represents extension of a point through one dimension of space. The point symbolizes the Self, the center of the Circle of Psyche. So, the extension of the point into space in some direction is the perfect symbol for the extension of the human will or agency. Understanding such things intellectually is helpful, to be sure, but explaining symbols in words misses how symbolism actually works. In fact, not understanding a symbol in words or abstract terms may be a better way to use symbols. If we are to make use of symbolic tools, they must

Wanderings: The Wand Is Everywhere

THE WAND IS the Appian Way of consciousness that runs from godhead to yourhead.

The wand is all things active; all things positive; all things protrusive and penetrating. The wand is the instrument of fatherhood; the phallus of creation; and the photons of sunlight. The wand is the hollow fennel stalk with which Prometheus brought the gift of fire (stolen from the gods) to humankind. The wand is firm; it is straight; it is singular. It is the undeviating Will of God—and ultimately, the Will of God must be the Will of the Magician.

The wand is nothing less than the pure, one-pointed purpose for which you have incarnated, and it is also the tool by which you must dispatch that sacred duty.

—Lon Milo DuQuette, *Homemade Magick*

become part of our inner being, internalized into the psyche on a level deeper than mere intellectual verbal understanding. They must be taken to heart (to use another symbol), known intuitively without picking them apart. The physical wand on your altar is the objective representation of your inner wand, which is your ability to act upon all the planes of existence. And it is this inner power that is actually the "tool"—the instrumentality of magic.

The Parts of a Wand

The wand is a symbol as a whole, and like many symbols it also has symbolic parts. Not all wands are constructed with these parts explicitly in a visual form but every wand possesses them. They are simply part of the geometry of the wand—and the line, its geometric shape. A line consists of two points in space connected. Thus it has two ends and a middle of variable length. One end is where it starts and the other is where it ends up. When it is grasped, the user takes up the origin point. It is convenient to use the terminology employed with bladed weapons and to refer to the rounded end in the hand as the pommel (from the French for apple), the handle as the hilt, the line itself as the shaft, and the ending point of the line, the point. In phallic terms, the pommel is the source of the seed of desire and the "point" is the end that emits that seed into the fertile body of the cosmos. The shaft is necessary so that the seed is planted where you want it to go and not simply dispersed everywhere. The seed is concentrated intention that has been wrapped up in symbols to give it structure. In a sense, a wand itself is a kind of spell: a symbolic structure created to manipulate spiritual energy.

The Pommel or Reservoir

On a sword or dagger the pommel is the rounded and weighted bit at the end that balances the blade. Magically, the rounded shape of the wand's originating end symbolizes the feminine or yin energy—that is potential energy held in reserve to be released. It may be shaped like an egg or an acorn, or may have a rounded stone set into it. Imagine a vessel filled with spiritual power in its purest form, unconditioned by desire except to act upon the cosmos magically. Held in the hand, this reservoir is filled by your will through the central energy point in your palm, which the Taoist wizards call the lao gong point. It contains part of your astral body, indeed part of the astral plane. It receives your energy.

It is generally understood that a wand should have a feminine and masculine end—negative and positive. These terms for polarity are drawn from electromagnetism and are confusing. A magic wand does not carry a current of electricity or generate a magnetic field with positive and negative poles. The etheric current and field is similar to what we study on the material plane as electromagnetic phenomena. But they are not the same thing. The analogy is confusing, because in discussing electromagnetism "positive" and "negative" refer to the direction of a current. It flows from positive (its source) to negative (wherever it is going)—or in other words, from presence to absence, from high pressure to low. When witches say that the pommel of a wand is feminine, that is right. But to then describe "feminine" as "negative" is contradictory. The feminine "pole" of a wand is the reservoir, the origin from which the current flows and therefore "positive" in electromagnetic terms.

The feminine is the material world, the rhythm of the heart and of Change in the world. Change with a capital C, meaning the whole matrix of dynamic forces, growth, solidity, fluidity, and the rest as manifested in the material plane. Another aspect of materiality that the pommel represents is gesture. As a witch makes a gesture with her wand, she puts into material form the astral desire and intention. The pommel is the earth element in the wand's structure, but cannot be thought of as "negative" or even "passive." It is a reservoir of potential etheric energy.

The Hilt

The hilt of a sword or dagger is where you grip it. Wands, not being used as cutting and thrusting weapons, do not require the same kind of hilt as a dagger, though the wrapping of the hilt of a wand with leather or decorating it with carvings is perfectly appropriate. The symbolism of the hilt can be understood in terms of the whole structure. Magically, the four parts of the wand correspond to the four elements, and the hilt represents water, which is the fluid of your etheric power flowing from your material body. Put another way, water, the element of the moon, is the representative in matter of the astral realm, which is all fluid. Fluidity is change. The astral plane is the fluid source of desires shaped into images. The hilt may be held lightly by the fingertips or firmly, but in each case the energy flows from your hand and the pommel through the hilt.

The Shaft

The shaft is the line extended toward its end point, and yet not really the end, for the true end of the line is the object of the spell, not just the end of the wand's physical body. The shaft corresponds to elemental air, which symbolizes thought. It is active, assertive, yang, luminous. The practice of spellcasting involves words and gestures as well as pure feelings and desires. We call them "spells" from the Old English word for "words," which we still find in spelling tests at school and spelling bees. It is this aspect of language and rational thought with words that is expressed by the element of air. As the ethereal energy of your hand rises from your unconscious depths (earth) to flow as moving energy (water), it is then shaped by your words and the incantation of the spell (air). Which leads us to fire.

The Point

The point of the wand corresponds to elemental fire. It may be simply tapered or it may be embellished with carving, or a crystal or other-pointed object in metal, bone, antler, etc. This part of your wand represents your power of agency. Fire is the heat of our blood and muscles, the instinctive urges we feel as passion. It is neither the rational conscious mind of elemental air, nor the unconscious source of wisdom in water. It is that aspect of our being we call spirit, the very life force itself upon which we draw to shape the world around us. And that is the point of magic.

In some cases the point of the wand is augmented with a crystal, an antler point, or a shape like an acorn or pinecone, meant to make it a phallic symbol, but it is more basically the pointing act, an act of direction. The acorn and pinecone on the end of a rod has been a phallic image since ancient times. The thyrsus of the Bacchantes was this kind of wand used in the Bacchanalian rites. A priapic wand was also made for rites of the Roman fertility god Priapus.

In sum, the elemental correspondences among the parts of a wand can be drawn as follows:

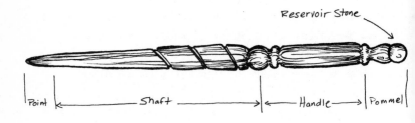

Reservoir Stone

Point | Shaft | Handle | Pommel

The parts of a wand

The following table will clarify the correspondences and their meaning for the structure and process of moving energy through a magic wand.

Table of Correspondences for Wand Parts

Part	Element	Gender	Psychic Power	Meaning
Pommel	Earth	Feminine Containing	Intuition	The physical and astral senses focused through the hand. Source of energy current.
Handle	Water	Feminine Filling	Feeling	The force of emotions and subjective evaluation to create relationships. Feeling and motion.
Shaft	Air	Masculine Projecting	Thought	The invisible organizing principle that uses symbols to define and give form and direction.
Point	Fire	Masculine Asserting	Action, will	The force of personal intention and desire to shape action. Do, go, be.

Wanderings: A Priapic Wand

NAMED FOR PRIAPIS, the Roman god of procreation, these sacred tools are most commonly made from a small branch topped with an acorn or crystal…The priapic wand can be used in fertility and sexual rites of any variety. If a woman wishes to get pregnant, for example, she can use this wand to project energy to her womb to give it a boost of fertility energy in preparation for a sacred sexual act, such as a Great Rite. If a woman (or a man!) is seeking a lover, the priapic wand can be placed on the altar in a variety of creative ways in order to project this energy out into the ethers to draw the right person close.

—Thuri Calafia, author of *The Initiate* and *The Dedicant*

The Vertical Wand or Staff

You may be asking—how do these wand parts apply to a staff, which, in addition to being longer, is also held differently? In fact, the staff can be held like a wand, with the tip pointing at the object of enchantment, for example, when casting a circle. The pommel of a staff is not a pommel like in a sword or dagger but instead is the top of the staff that is held upward. The handle is wherever the hand rests when carrying it (or two hands when lifting it to point). Wands are typically carried in this attitude, which is to say, point down, reservoir of power up. With the rod pointing to the earth, its power is not directed anywhere except into the ground; sort of a safety. At the same time, the vertical situation of the rod emphasizes the symbolic direction we think of when we think of the higher planes. The source of power is both earth and the heavens, as when lightning strikes down and up in the same instant, forming a circuit.

You may have read that the human spine embodies what Kabbalists have called the Middle Pillar. Hindu yogis speak of the kundalini power that can be awakened to run up and down the spine's pranic meridians. Suffice to say here that the vertical position of a staff aligns the rod's power in the same way, turning it into a representation of the planes and the construction of the cosmos. It is the Norse world tree, Yggdrasil, or the sacred tree of Being.

Some smaller wands are also used in the vertical position, held like a scepter. Their tops are decorated and the shaft may be divided into the colors of the planes or the planets to indicate that the wand embraces all levels of being. Similarly, a wand used in the tradition of the Hermetic Order of the Golden Dawn, which is modeled on ancient Egyptian magic, takes the signs of the zodiac and gives each a different color to create a spectrum (with the addition of black and white). From top to bottom, its colors are white, red, reddish orange, orange, yellow-orange, gold, yellow, green, blue-green, blue, indigo, purple, violet, black. Black and white are universals. Each of the other colors corresponds to a constellation. The lotus on top is a symbol of spiritual openness.

The thyrsus or phallic wand is familiar to witches. It is a wand sometimes held upright and sometimes pointed at an object. Usually it has a pinecone on top, which gives it a phallic appearance but also captures the fertility of the coniferous tree and its cone filled with seeds. The evergreen conifer symbolizes Life.

Gerald Gardner in *The Gardnerian Book of Shadows* describes the use of the wand in the sabbat of summer solstice as follows:

- Form circle. Invoke, purify. Cauldron is placed before altar filled with water, wreathed with summer flowers. The people, men and women alternately, stand round circle. High priestess stands in north, before cauldron, holding raised wand, which should be phallic or tipped with a pinecone (anciently the thyrsus) or a riding pole or a broomstick, invokes the sun.

- After the invocation, the wand exchanges hands between the female and male powers:

- High priestess draws invoking pentacle on magus with wand. Magus comes forward sunwise and takes wand with kiss, plunges wand into cauldron and holds it upright, saying, "The spear to the cauldron, the lance to the grail, spirit to flesh, man to woman, sun to earth." He salutes high priestess over cauldron, then rejoins people, still bearing wand.

- After this, the magus or high priest bears the wand throughout the dancing and procession.

Whether it symbolizes the planetary powers, the life force of the earth, or the connection between earth and sky, the wand or staff carries power by means of its symbolic meaning. It is not a lightning rod that conducts electricity simply

Wanderings: A Wisteria Wand

THE WAND I use most often was given to me by my father. He was forever picking up interesting sticks and seed pods for me in the garden, and one day came inside with a beautifully spiraling wisteria branch. I had just begun exploring magical work in earnest, and I was thrilled to find that the branch was the exact measure of my forearm to the tip of my middle finger.

Having no experience in woodworking, I sanded the wand as best I could, then rubbed it with a candle stub and repeatedly passed it through a flame to melt the wax into the surface. By some miracle it didn't scorch, and I've been using it to create sacred spaces ever since.

The winding nature of Wisteria makes this an excellent celebratory wand. The times the wand feels most powerful is in the spring and early summer, or anytime ritual is near a body of fresh water. The circles cast with it have a wild and lusty quality, conducive to bouts of joy and creative expression. However, it is not a "surgical" wand, i.e., I don't try to perform precise energy direction with it. The transmission of energy tends to be in multiple tendrils or ribbons, rather than as a focused stream—it's messy, expansive, and I love it!

—Catriona McDonald, author of *The Druid's Well* blog

because it is made of iron; it is a conductor of ethereal energy because the symbol draws out your intention to change the world from your mind into the matrix of energy underlying all material things. In other words, the power of a wand comes from your own mind, but its symbolism acts as the visible connection between your thoughts and the world.

For witch or mage, a symbol is not simply a bit of ink or carving. It is a magical and living entity, active as soon as it is touched by the magical will, so choose your symbols carefully and contemplate their meaning long and hard so that you are fully aware of everything they imply and convey.

Wood, Bone,
Metal, Stone

𝕿raditionally, wands are made of wood. In the stories of the old Druids, these wizards would take up a branch of birch, carve some symbols on it, and cast a spell. Druid wands are referred to as if they were tools Druids carried about all the time—and as Druid comes from *druidecht,* which is most often simply translated as "magic," the term "Druid wand" just means "magic wand." Likewise, the title "Druid" can most simply be translated "wizard." Both men and women could be Druids in the societies of ancient Britain and Ireland (and presumably elsewhere in the Celtic-speaking world of the time).

It is thought by Philip Carr-Gomm, Chosen Chief of the Order of Bards, Ovates and Druids, that the class of Druids called Ovates or Vates (seers or soothsayers) were those who practiced the arts of healing, herbalism, divination, and spell-work (see Carr-Gomm, *Druidcraft*). After the Romans wiped out the Druid college at the isle of Mona, it is possible that the Vates became the cunning folk who came to be known as "witches" in English.

Despite the tradition of wood wands, there are some prominent wandmakers today who make their magic wands out of pewter or other metals, interwoven with crystals. Metals give the advantage of being castable into intricate shapes. On the down side, few witches have the skills necessary to make such a wand themselves. Even in a wood wand, incorporating metals requires knowledge of how to handle them. The most popular metal to incorporate in a wand is copper, which can be done fairly easily using wire available at craft stores and winding it around the wand. Copper is the metal of the Goddess Venus, the goddess of love. She is the maiden in the triple goddess—maiden, mother, crone.

Silver is also a splendid metal to incorporate if you can afford it, as this metal is sacred to the moon, who represents all the mysteries of womanhood. Some wandmakers include all seven metals to correspond to the seven planets. This cannot really be done without substitutions, because the metal of Saturn is lead (poisonous) and the metal of Mercury is mercury or quicksilver (poisonous and liquid at room temperature). The metal of Mars is iron, which is a fidgety metal where magic is concerned. There are differing opinions. Some say iron is great because it can be magnetized. Others point out that iron tends to have strange (usually bad) effects on the denizens of the otherworlds, which is why iron is used so often in spells designed to keep away mischievous or malevolent otherworld entities. That is what your athame is for—banishing and protection.

While some ceremonial schools of magic think that having all seven of the planetary metals draws a kind of universal wholeness into a magical implement, my own feeling is that only one or two metals ought to be included in a wand unless it is built for a very specific purpose. Ceremonial magicians make very fancy wands to be used by different officers in their magical lodges. Each is symbolic of some magical principle and the powers of the particular officer who wields it. For witches and Druids, however, who do not go in for the revival of ancient Egyptian magic and that sort of thing, simple is better.

Clay is also used by some wandmakers, especially as a sculptable medium for holding stones and crystals. Natural clay would be tricky to use for this purpose, as it would have to be fired to be durable. Sculpey clay and other such products that can be hardened without high heat are better suited, but not natural substances. If you do not care about your wand being all-natural, then that is not a problem. Nor would I suggest that it impairs the function of the wand—the only way it would do so is if the materials mattered to you personally. Clay offers the benefits of sculpture where carving would be difficult.

On the other hand, Aleister Crowley said in his *Liber ABA*:

> The wand is not a wand if it has something sticking to it which is not an essential part of itself. If you wish to invoke Venus, you do not succeed if there are traces of Saturn mixed up with it.

So consider the esoteric forces at work in your materials.

Bone or antler can be used to spectacular effect and by a master carved with marvelous detail. Use of such animal materials brings the spirit of the animal into the wand. If you are a vegetarian this might not be desirable. But including something of the animal kingdom in your wand along with wood and stones will draw together the three major kingdoms—animal, vegetable, and mineral—to unite with your own spirit, representing the human kingdom. Including an astral core of a phoenix feather or unicorn hair accomplishes the same thing imaginally.

A general-purpose wand should not have too many different influences flowing through it. However, the amount of symbolism you include is entirely according to your own taste and style. If it works for you, that is all that matters. There are no rules when it comes to making wands. In fact, the wand is only useful if it works as a clear symbol and focus for your will. As a quick read, though, most spellbooks will tell you that nobody needs a wand to do magic. Your hands will do just fine. The advantage of the wand is the symbolic meaning it lends to the magical action. Put simply, it helps to have something to wave around and point at things, in the same way a conductor's baton is helpful.

However, that said, I do not think the power and value of a wand lies only in its sigils, runes, or its phallic symbolism, or its connection to royal scepters. The deeper power of a wooden wand lies in the spirit of the tree that resides in it—its dryad. Each kind of tree has magical properties that reflect the character of its dryad. This is old Druid lore and folklore handed down for centuries. I offer here only a thumbnail synopsis of the magical properties of trees, and of those, only the most common in northern climes. Every tree is magical and the best way to select your own branch is to know the trees around you, where you live. They are the ones to which you will have the closest spiritual connection, and the ones with whom you can communicate to ask for permission to use a branch. Sometimes, however, the branch will be a gift that falls in your path when wandering far from home.

Wanderings: A Blood Wand

A BRANCH, FROM a special tree you love, as long as the distance from elbow to third fingertip, taken under a full moon, which you pay for with one drop of your blood... rowan, oak, elder, willow, blackthorn, hazel, mistletoe... elderberry. Dig out a little hole in one end of the branch and stuff it with a piece of cotton and a drop of your menstrual blood. Seal with candle wax droppings. Put... a pentagram at the top and bottom. Consecrate it in the name of Diana with water, wine, fire, incense and oil and new moon time.

—Zsuzsanna Budapest, *The Holy Book of Women's Mysteries*

Magical Properties of Trees

The magical properties of trees, stones, and crystals have been studied by many witches and mages through the ages. The following is in no way intended to substitute for reading the many good books on the subject, nor for doing your own hands-on research with the actual trees and minerals. These brief descriptions will give you a sense of what different types of wood may be used for. Any wood can be used for general purpose magery, but some trees are more suited to particular kinds of actions. Likewise, stones and crystals can be used for magery in themselves or as part of a wand. When incorporated into a wand their properties meld and coalesce with those of the wood dryad and any magical animal core you may desire to include.

Alder

KEY: *Preserving*

Soft and easily carved, alder is famous in bridge-building for its ability to resist rotting when submerged in water. It was used in Scotland to build crannochs, fortified villages floating on alder logs in lochs and connected to the land by a defensible bridgework. Most of Venice, Italy, is built on pilings of alder (Kendall, "Mythology"). Alder is a tree of bridging, crossing over, and connection to other worlds, both in its use to make bridges crossing waters and in its use submerged in water. Water is the element most connected to the Celtic oth-erworld of faerie. The alder has been revered because its sap turns red, like blood, when exposed to air. This characteristic is also the source of some negative folklore, suggesting that alder is dangerous, which might also have been because alder woods were boggy and treacherous. Alder is a wood sacred to bards and musicians because it is an excellent wood for mak-ing pipes and whistles. It makes an excellent water wand, and is especially suited to oracular magic, seership, dreamwork, and spells for preservation, concealment, crossing, emotional bridges, and bridging the worlds. It is also well-suited to magic of music and enchantment, and spells against flooding or to protect from water damage or drowning.

Ash

KEY: *Journeying*

Prized for its straight and prominent grain and elasticity, ash wood makes a bold and sturdy wand. Norse myth associates this tree with the World Tree Yggdrasil. Oak, ash, and thorn are often grouped as sacred magical trees in Pagan traditions. Ash is direct, straight-grained, the very embodiment of the ray of will. It is well-suited for shamanic magic traveling between worlds, protection, the search for knowledge to enhance one's skills at any art or craft. It is suited to the magic of wells and caves, earth as the vessel of water, water encompassing earth. Also, working with plant roots, magic of female sovereignty, and—because of its links to water—weather working and dowsing. Ash's combination of earth and water make it ideal for healing magic.

Apple
KEY: *Singing*

The core of the apple fruit in cross section is a pentagram, a five-pointed star. This shape is associated with the five senses or the four elements with the addition of the fifth—the quintessence. The pentagram acts to protect and bless. Celtic bards are described in legend as carrying apple branches laden with silver bells as a symbol of their office and magical power. The mythical Silver Bough and its golden apples provided entry to the realm of faerie. Apple wands are especially suited to opening the doorways into otherworlds, spells to do with travel, deception, or the unmasking of it, illumination, love, harmony, and beauty, harvest, abundance, and magic of rescue and recovery, and the defeat of dark, devouring powers. Apple evokes poetic inspiration and the power to enchant through words and music. It brings the otherworld into this world.

Birch
KEY: *Beginning*

In Celtic Ogham Lore, birch is the tree of beginnings, a harbinger of youth and springtime. It is also sacred to bards. The bards of old learned memory, grace, language, and the entire

lore of their people. Such knowledge is the foundation of imaginal power upon which one can build the magic, creative, and
healing arts. Birch is also a tree with great powers to purify
and discipline, to create the new forest in service to the great
trees that will come after, such as the oak, ash, and maple.
Birch groves bespeak a young forest and so birch is linked to
youth and all things that are the foundations of larger things
to come. A birch wand is especially suited to magic of new
beginnings, spells of youth and fresh starts, bardic enchantment, creativity, procreation, birth, renewal and rebirth, purification, and spells for discipline and service.

Beech

KEY: *Learning*

The stately beech is another tree sacred to the sun. The leaves
of the beech turn on their stalks to face the sun. It can thus
be considered sacred to the Greek Apollo, and to Celtic Lugh,
Ogma, and Belinos, each of whom is associated with the bril-
liance of the sun. The sun represents the deep source of all
life and beauty at the center of the planetary system. It is
a symbol of the Self, the deep center of the human psyche.
The beech nut, like the oak's acorn, is a food source eaten by
humans and their pigs.

Jacqueline Memory Paterson, in her book on the lore of
trees, says that beech is called "Mother of the Woods" for its
nurturing qualities. The tree is most associated in Celtic tra-

dition with wisdom and books. Beech is a beautifully grained wood, golden in color, and it takes fine carving well. It is well-suited to all forms of solar and positive magic, the enhancement of creativity, learning, and the search for information. The wizard seeking magical books and learning will wish to employ a beech wand.

Cherry

KEY: *Desiring*

The cherry tree, like the Holly, is sacred to the spirit of the hunt and of protection, that quality that in classical astrology is the spirit of Mars. Called Ares by the Greeks, and often identified with Teutates among the Celtic tribes, Mars should not be thought of as strictly a god of war. Such divinities served as patrons of the warrior class in societies that identify a knightly class or caste. The class of warriors in tribal societies are the protectors of the tribe.

Cherry wood is red in hue and darkens with age and exposure to sunlight, like blood. It is imbued with the power of doing, achievement, and self-assertion over obstacles and critics. Cherry wands are especially well-suited to invocations and blessings of sacred fires, spells of finding, hunting, conflict, war, competition, communion with animals, unification of groups or tribes, mating, the balance of assertive and receptive forces, and the amplification of magical will generally. Cherry can also make a very powerful healing wand for injuries of body or soul sustained in conflict, loss, or from the breakup of a passionate attachment.

Elder
KEY: *Regenerating*

The Hyldemoer or "Elder Mother" was considered to be a spirit indwelling in the elder tree, who "worked strong earth magic." Certain North American tribes also believe that elder is the mother of the human race (Paterson, *Tree Wisdom*, 279). Elder is a famous "witch tree"—that is, one of the trees that witches are supposed to turn themselves into. It is one of the trees that acts as a conduit to the faerie realm, especially if a person lies down under one and falls asleep, seduced by the fragrance of its flowers.

Elder is used for the handles of witches' broomsticks. The pith at the core of its branches makes it well-suited for the sort of wand design that includes a crystal point and a reservoir pommel stone, or an inclusion in the center, if the pith is removed. For wand designs that include a magnetized wire running through the center, elder would be a good choice. Elder is particularly adapted for healing and is an excellent choice for a wand of protection. It is a good choice for ceremonial work with mother goddesses.

Elm

KEY: *Containing*

One of the tallest ancient forest trees, graceful in its chalice shape, limbs spreading up to the sky. Elm is sacred to the Great Goddess in her form as Wise Grandmother. One of elm's nicknames is "elven" for its connection to the elves (the English or Germanic name for the good people of the Hollow Hills). As such, elm is associated with burial mounds and with the doorways to faerie. Elm's spirit is majestic and expansive, rooted and wise. Its wood is coarse-grained and staining brings out the patterns of the grain beautifully. It is a tough, hard wood. Elm is well-suited to wands that will be used for earthworking or invocation of the Great Mother. Also for healing, fertility, gardening, rebirth, destiny, wisdom, passage from one life (or phase of life) to another, metamorphosis, and endurance.

Hawthorn

KEY: *Guarding*

Hawthorn, or whitethorn, is sacred to the white hart of Arthurian romance who leads the adventurer into the otherworld through the ancient darkness of the forest. Hawthorn's vibration is that of the Green Man, personification of the wild and of the union of human, animal, and vegetable fertility. We see the same union in the figure of Cernunnos, the antlered stag god. The donning of antlers by shamans unites man and beast, upper and lower worlds, spirit and body. With its twisted branches and sharp thorns, hawthorn is a tree of defense and it holds the power of lightning, the Promethean fire stolen from Zeus. Loremasters say a hawthorn wand can detect the presence of magic, because it is a tree through which magical powers enter the manifest world from beyond. Thus it is highly suited to projecting power over other kinds of magic—counter jinxes and counter curses, but also controlling the accuracy of all spells. Hawthorn is well-suited for wands of protection and strength, spells of control or warding, sending, detection, concealment, weatherworking. Hawthorn flowers are the "May" referred to in association with Beltane. These white blossoms celebrate the rebirth of the Green Man and the renewal of fertility in the earth. A Beltane wand should really be made of hawthorn.

Hazel

Key: *Understanding*

Hazel is the tree of the White Goddess, the Queen of Heaven. In my practice and belief, the goddess of stars is Arianrhod, a Welsh goddess intimately associated with wands. Her name means "the silver wheel," which may refer to the full moon or to Corona Borealis, a constellation considered to be her home in the sky. Hazel wands carry her power. In the Celtic legends, hazelnuts feed the Salmon of Wisdom in the deep pool of Segais, where it lives, the otherworld source of the River Boyne in Ireland. This watery association is important to remember in hazel. The Well of Segais is surrounded by the nine hazels of inspiration. The hazelnuts ripen and fall into the pool where the Salmon eats them. The well at the center of creation is also the heart chakra—center of love and attraction, and thus hazel wands are especially suited for anything having to do with love.

Hazel wood is close-grained, white, and takes detailed carving beautifully. It is well-suited to magic of wisdom, beauty, charm, stars, summoning, attraction, and creativity. Its strong associations with the shee-folk makes it ideal for wands of communication used in collaboration with the folk of faerie— in a much lighter and more cerebral way than blackthorn, or even hawthorn.

Holly

KEY: *Penetrating*

Holly and oak form a pair in the lore of the Celts, for each represents as half of the year. The story is told how the Holly King and the Oak King would battle each other twice a year to determine who was stronger. At Midsummer, when the oaks are in full leaf, they dominate the forests, and the smaller holly trees are lost in the abundance of the Oak King's splendor. But after the sun turns again southward, starting its waning journey, the Holly King grows stronger each day. As an

91

Wanderings: A Companion in Magic and Life

MY WAND EVOKES the unique and personal relationship I have with a particular tree—in my case, a holly. She is stout and tall. I grew her from seed; we are friends, the holly and I. The wand, or *hudlath* as it is called in my native Welsh tongue, is more than simply a tool that projects my will; it is an ally in magic.

In Druidry there is much emphasis on sacred relationships, and the connection a magician has with his or her wand expresses that. When I take to my wand, I bring into ritual or an act of magic the entire story of the relationship between the holly and I. This connection bridges the materialistic chasm between human nature and wild nature. Wherever I am in the world, my wand roots me to the ground; to call her to me centers my spirit and brings the subtle world into focus.

To have a deep connection with a wand is to never be alone in magic; to grasp it firmly in the hand is to embrace the power of that tree. My wand contains more than simply the story of a holly that I grew; it also contains the memory of her ancestors. She is plain, unpolished, and yet within her is contained the story of my life and hers.

—Kristoffer Hughes, author of
From the Cauldron Born,
The Book of Celtic Magic, etc.

evergreen tree, holly remains green and bold when the oak leaves begin to fall, and at the winter solstice, the Holly King has triumphed. The oaks stand naked and apparently dead while the holly trees now show their red berries upon their spear-sharp leaves.[2] Despite its association with winter and the underworld, Holly is one of the most fiery of woods, from the standpoint of the philosophical elements. Holly wands are powerfully protective, good against evil spirits, poisons, angry elementals, and lightning. They are also particularly good for averting fear, and so for allowing courage to emerge, in dream magic, and to overthrow old authorities and achieve success in all endeavors. Holly's energy moves us to progress to a new stage of development. Holly wood is very fine-grained, hard, and smooth, almost ivory in color if it is not stained. It is a truly exquisite wood for wands.

Linden

Key: *Attracting*

The linden, also called basswood and lime-tree, is the tree most sacred to the power of love. The linden tree's flowers look like shooting stars and have an intoxicating perfume in summer. Linden wood is laden with the power of attraction that underlies love, infatuation, musical harmony, and the

---

2 It is actually the female holly trees that bear the red berries in fall and winter, so perhaps it should be the Holly *Queen!*

very fabric of the cosmos in such forces as magnetism, adhesion, and gravity. It is a very lightweight, airy, and smooth wood, excellent for carving. Its wood is also fibrous and tough and these fibers were used by Native Americans to make strong ropes, something that is also symbolic of its power to attract, hold, and bind.

Wands of linden are excellent for work with goddesses of love, including those that give their love to their devotees, such as Arianrhod and Athene, as well as Aphrodite. It is enduring love, not flighty or quickly passing. The ancient Germanic tribes used light and strong linden wood for shields—shielding from hate and rancor. Linden wands are especially suited to spells of creation and transmutation, illumination, love, attraction, binding, obligation, healing wounds, enhancement of beauty, peace, and acts of enchantment generally. It is particularly ill-suited for cursing or any magic that aims at division or separation.

Maple
Key: *Changing*

Maple is sacred to the Autumnal Equinox because of its fiery autumnal colors but also to spring when its flowing sap gives us maple syrup. Its colors are a bold celebration of the cycle of death and rebirth as something joyous, not sad. Poised on the equinox, it is linked to both Libra and Virgo, air and earth. In North America, especially in its northern forests, the maple

Wood, Bone, Metal, Stone

is a dominant tree with many varieties, including the sugar maple. Wands of maple wood are beautiful and richly colored and are associated with the life-giving sap of the trees, providing food and sweetness for those who treat it with respect and care.

Maple is a strong, hard wood, sometimes rebellious and tough, sometimes more gentle. It has a beautiful smooth grain. It is hard, yet excellent for carving. Maple wands are especially well-suited to spells of control, finding, binding, transformation, creation, revolution, rebirth, poetry, beauty, harvest, healing, and abundance. Its key—"changing"—expresses this universal power within nature. The maple wand would be my choice for a celebratory instrument at the sabbat of Mabon or for operations requiring the mingling of air and earth energies.

Oak

KEY: *Opening*

The most powerful and sacred of Druid trees, oak resonates with the constellation Leo by virtue of it solar associations in folklore. It holds power to draw lightning or the bolt of inspiration. The sun, which rules Leo, is the source of life and light. Oak symbolizes all solar heroes, those who venture out from their homelands to achieve great deeds and bring home wondrous treasures after voyaging into the underworld. Oak traditionally has provided not only one of the most durable woods for construction and fuel, but also the acorn on which our ancestors fed their pigs. Oak is one of the longest-lived trees, thus embodying great wisdom as well as strength. The word Druid is thought to derive from the Old Celtic words for oak and wisdom. As the wizard-wood, there is no more magical wood for wandmaking; it is especially noted for enhancing the endurance of spells against time and for counter-spells. The acorn resembles a helmeted head and so relates to the crown chakra, the seat of spiritual power and wisdom. Natural branches of oak are often twisted and gnarly and have thick, rough bark and a coarse, dark grain that can be tough to carve and does not easily carry detailed figures. Oak is a hard and heavy wood, especially suited to wands used for operations of leadership and wise rule, personal sovereignty, authority, power, protection, sealing or opening doors, endurance, patience, prudence, fertility, and abundance.

Rowan

KEY: *Quickening*

The rowan's flowers and berries bear the pentagram, symbol of the five elements and five senses. The pentagram's use as a sign of protection makes rowan an excellent choice for wands used to banish and protect. Also called "witchen" and "witchbane," rowan has been considered the enemy of all evil witchery. A wand of this wood protects against one's being carried off to faerie against one's will. A tree of astral vision and protection, particularly good for warding off evil spirits, rowan also is said to avert storms and lightning, and to bring peace. Fine-grained and creamy smooth, rowan wood is a delight to carve. It is especially suited for wands to invoke form and order, ritual, growth, fertility, protection, rebirth, women's autonomy, poetry, metalwork, stone carving, weaving and spinning, and geomancy, or work with ley lines.

Walnut

KEY: *Illuminating*

Sacred to the Lord of Winds and Lightning, Walnut partakes of both air and fire. It is perhaps the consummate wood for weather magic. In Gaul this spirit was called Taranis, Lord of Thunder. Jupiter and Zeus are the Roman and Greek gods, as is Indra in the Vedic pantheon of India, Thor in the Norse. Many gods and goddesses are associated with the heavens as either sky, storm, or sun deities. It is this elemental power of air and rain that we find within the walnut tree. The shape of the walnut tree's nut connects it to the head—it looks like a brain when opened, right down to the left and right hemispheres. It should come as no surprise that walnut is attuned to the crown chakra, and to mysticism. This is to say that walnut's power includes the ability to open one to the fullest dimensions of one's being. If we look to Jupiter we find that in astrology this planet governs all forms of expansion and increase: expansion of wealth, horizons, the mind, the feelings. Walnut wood ranges from light to very dark brown in color and is easy to carve. In a wand, it is especially suited for wind and weather magic, spells of expansion and fertility, vortices, enhancement of the powers of breath, spells to conjure or avert lightning, hurricanes, or cyclones. Also for spells of teleportation, astral travel, and inspiration.

Willow

KEY: *Weaving*

Sacred to the moon, willow is associated with the many goddesses of the moon, including Diana, Selene, Artemis, Circe, Hecate, and Cerridwen. Willow is distinctly a wood of the water element, often growing at water's edge, and so it is good for dowsing and other forms of seership. Willow has been used for rain-making, funerary rites, love spells, easing childbirth, fertility, healing, and spells of glamour and bewitchment. Willow osiers have been used since earliest times to make wickerwork and this wood is also used to make the sound boxes of harps. It is a remarkably flexible wood and regenerates quickly when coppiced, demonstrating its powers of healing and rebirth. Its bark is widely known as a pain reliever, the source of the main ingredient in aspirin (salicylic acid, from the Latin *salix*, willow). As the consummate witch-wood, a willow wand invokes and guides cycles of change, relationships, and female rites of passage. It is the perfect wand wood for the ritual of drawing down the moon and is suited to magic of the dark moon and night—acts of concealment, secrecy, and germination—as well as magic of the full moon (and any other phase for that matter). As a water-wood, willow is the wood of choice for stir-wands used in potion-making. As apple embodies harmony, willow embodies melody and combination, weaving together diverse strands of reality into containers of magic.

Yew

KEY: *Remembering*

Yew is sacred to the Celtic god Arawn, the Gray Lord of the Dead and Master of Possibility, and also to the Morrigan. Great Queen Maeve is another of the Morrigan's many names, also spelled Mabh in Irish. In several guises, Maeve is the goddess overseeing the death of heroes, the lifeblood, and the doorway death presents between the worlds. We may also think of the Greek god Hermes's office as psychopomp (guide of souls), leading the souls of the dead into the new world of the afterlife. The evergreen yew is attuned to travel between the worlds, changes of state between life now and life with our ancestors. This is why yew trees appear in so many British and Irish churchyards beside the graves. Yew's toxic berries give further associations with death and shamanic trance. Yew wands are especially suited to spells of transformation, illusion, astral travel, mediumship, necromancy, conjuration of helpful spirits, guides and ancestors, and also spells to bestow knowledge, eloquence, or persuasion. Obviously, a yew wand

Wanderings: Levi's Fashion Advice for Wizards

IN DESCRIBING THE regalia of a magician, Eliphas Levi declares that on Sunday (the day of the sun) he should carry in his right hand a golden wand, set with a ruby or chrysolite; on Monday (the day of the moon) he should wear a collar of three strands consisting of pearls, crystals, and selenites; on Tuesday (the day of Mars) he should carry a wand of magnetized steel and a ring of the same metal set with an amethyst, on Wednesday (the day of Mercury) he should wear a necklace of pearls or glass beads containing mercury, and a ring set with an agate; on Thursday (the day of Jupiter) he should carry a wand of glass or resin and wear a ring set with an emerald or a sapphire; on Friday (the day of Venus) he should carry a wand of polished copper and wear a ring set with a turquoise and a crown or diadem decorated with lapis lazuli and beryl; and on Saturday (the day of Saturn) he should carry a wand ornamented with onyx stone and wear a ring set with onyx and a chain about the neck formed of lead.

—Manly P. Hall, *The Secret Teachings of All Ages*

is also well-suited to spells related to death and grieving. It is the wood of choice if you are making a wand to celebrate Samhuinn and gain contact with your ancestors. Used regularly, it will change your consciousness to let you fully realize that you are always already living with the presence of your ancestors.

Stones and Crystals

A magic wand can certainly be made without the addition of stones or crystals. However, adding a representative of the mineral kingdom ties a wand more closely to that place where matter and energy combine. The use of a crystal or cut stone point in a wand is a practice derived from the use of crystals in healing work, especially with regard to the chakras. Crystals are valued for their ability to focus energy and cleanse or unblock the flows in the astral and ethereal bodies. Many crystals are powerful fluid condensers—substances that "condense" or intensify the flow of etheric fluid (see Bardon, *Initiation into Hermetics*).

The most frequent choice for a crystal point is clear quartz. Other varieties of quartz—such as smoky quartz, rutilated quartz, tourmalinated quartz, rose quartz, and the crystals amethyst, citrine, and so forth—each have their peculiar qualities that will be added to the energies passing through them. Inclusion of a citrine crystal, for example, can lend an overall solar quality to the energy transmitted by the wand. There is not likely to be anything contrary in that, unless your purpose is to use the wand to work with the energy of the moon. The wand will still work, of course, governed by your will, but it will not be as suitable as would be, for example, a willow wand with milky quartz. However, a few combinations might prove contradictory, such as using a wand with an amethyst point to cast a spell of intoxication over someone, since amethyst is known for averting intoxication. But such contradictions are very specific.

From a physical standpoint, if a crystal point is to be included, it is good to balance its weight with a reservoir stone. In such cases the choice of crystal and stone may strive for harmony or it may strive for the union of opposites. If the latter is the case, one might, for example, balance a clear quartz point with a reservoir stone of jet or black obsidian. If harmony between the two minerals is sought, a combination, such as moonstone in the pommel with milky quartz in the point, could serve to provide a harmonious feminine energy. A point of cut lapis lazuli might be harmonized with a pommel stone of carnelian, the former having an abundance of essential air and the latter essential fire. Both air and fire are masculine, so in this example a harmonious balance of masculine energies is given to the wand.

What follows are very brief notes on the qualities of the most common minerals used in magic wands (not including precious stones like diamond and ruby, which are generally out of most witches' budgets). Much fuller descriptions and discussions of the magical properties of stones may be found in my book *Wandlore: The Art of Crafting the Ultimate Magical Tool* or at my website: www.bardwood.com.

Agate

Agate is a type of quartz known as chalcedony with banded patterns of color. It has powers of protection, victory, attracting love, promoting fertility in crops, turning away lightning or evil spirits, finding buried treasure, curing insomnia, and giving pleasant dreams.

Tree Agate

Usually white with black, brown, or green branchlike inclusions. White is purity and light while the branches emulate the many paths that govern our choices. It harmonizes with the energies of Libra for the choices made and the balance of probability.

Moss Agate

Green with bands in shades of blue and green. Powers of eloquence and persuasion, fertility, magnetism, and eternal life, healing, meditation, scrying, astral travel, and speaking with spirit guides. These outcomes depend upon the careful manipulation of the delicate intertwined fibers of causality.

Amber

Solidified sunlight, it cannot be called a stone because it is really resin with natural electrical properties that inspires attraction and sensuality, making it useful in love spells. In his book *Initiation into Hermetics*, Franz Bardon incorporates amber into his fluid condensers (more later about this). Used for travel through time, imagination of the past, solar work, creative and generative forces.

Amethyst

A kind of quartz, purple or lilac in color. Averts intoxication, protects from losing control of oneself, from false infatuation with an idea or a person. It is associated with the third eye, clairvoyance, prescience, and the ability to see through illusions. Also healing, amethyst calms mental disorders and balances chakras.

Aventurine

A green type of quartz, sometimes called Indian jade, aventurine is a stone used to release anxieties, which inspires independence, positive attitudes, and good health. Gives balance and calm. Enhances creative visualization, writing, art, and music. Aventurine attracts prosperity, love, and unexpected adventures or opportunities.

Bloodstone

Green with red flecks like blood, an opaque green jasper. It links the root and heart chakras, stimulating kundalini. Guards against deceptions and preserves health, creates prosperity, and strengthens self-confidence. Can lengthen life, give fame, aid invisibility, remove obstacles, control spirits, and help in court cases.

Carnelian

Orange or reddish, related to bloodstone and moss agate, carnelian protects against the "evil eye" and is used to fulfill all desires. Sacred to Venus, it speeds all manifestations, revitalizes and aligns the physical and spiritual bodies, strengthens concentration, increases the sense of self-worth, brings success, and balances creative and organizational abilities.

Citrine

A clear, pale yellow variety of quartz that can be used for reservoir stones and as wand points. Sacred to the sun and Scorpio, it protects against intoxication, evil thoughts, overindulgence, plagues, epidemics, and sudden misfortune of a physical nature generally. Aligns one's ego with one's higher self.

Fluorite

More soft and breakable than quartz, fluorite may be green, purple, yellow, or even colorless. Its most well-known property is "fluorescence" or glowing in the dark. It holds astral light and is connected to Pisces and Capricorn. Fluorite grounds excessive energy and elevates one's senses into the etheric body. A powerful healing stone for all chakras.

Hematite

Dark iron-gray with a metallic luster, hematite is a blood-red color when powdered. Sacred to Mars, it is used to gain favorable hearings or judgments, to win petitions before those in authority, and to protect warriors. Associated with Aries and Aquarius, it energizes the etheric body and gives optimism, will, and courage.

Jade

Best known as apple green in color, Jade gives precognitive dreams. Associated with Aries, Gemini, and Libra, jade strengthens the heart, kidneys, and immune system, increases fertility, cleanses ethereally, balances the emotions, dispels negativity, and gives courage and wisdom.

Jasper

A variety of chalcedony that is fine-grained, it may take many colors but is often red. Good for bringing rain and healing. Balances all chakras, stabilizes energy, and protects from negativity. Drives away evil spirits, hallucinations, and nightmares, jasper is generally a grounding stone and is sacred to Jupiter.

Lapis Lazuli

Lapis lazuli is a combination of dark blue azurite, hauynite, sodalite, diopside, white streaks of calcite, and specks of gold pyrite. Sacred to the Egyptian goddess Isis, the planet Jupiter, and the throat chakra. Removes painful memories from the astral body. A stone of good fortune, it helps release tension and anxiety and enhances astral awareness.

Malachite

Dark green with swirls and stripes of lighter green, which come from copper. Sacred to Venus, Minerva, and Cerridwen. Helps understand animal languages, protection, and revitalizing the body and mind. Repels evil spirits, inspires tolerance and flexibility, opens communication, and stabilizes energy. A psychic mirror reflecting whatever is put into it.

Moonstone

Milky white or pink opalescent, it carries the power of dreams, astral travel, and openness to the lunar sphere of manifestation. Moonstone has healing qualities, especially as applied to the astral body. Sacred to Aradia, Diana, Luna, Selene, and Arianrhod. Moonstone has full moon energies, distinct from the darker energy of the new moon.

Quartz Crystal

The most generally powerful magical amplifier, quartz crystal is most common for wand points. When rounded, they also make excellent reservoir stones. Ruled by the moon, quartz crystal gives access to the astral worlds and is well-suited to meditation, communication with spirit guides, telepathy, clairvoyance, and visualization. Besides clear quartz crystal, there are several special varieties, as follows.

Rose Quartz

Pink quartz, called the "love stone," aids in healing the emotions, the development of compassion, and reducing stress and anxiety. Resonant specifically to the heart chakra. The union of spirit and blood, it is the stone to choose for love spells, but recognize also that the power of love underlies all positive magic.

Smoky Quartz

Grayish brown, it aids in discrimination and is attuned to the root chakra. It aids grounding and centering, and breaks up energy blockages and resulting negativity. Transforms dreams into reality by bringing them into the material plane. Sacred to Pluto, Arawn, and other underworld deities.

Milky Quartz

Translucent to opaque white, draws upon the power of the moon to nurture and heal. It opens the doors of perception into the higher worlds and attracts good spirit guides for travel within the lunar sphere. Sacred to the goddesses Diana, Artemis, Isis, Arianrhod, and Cerridwen. Promotes all magic to do with mothers and their children, home, family, emotions, moods, and feelings.

Rutilated Quartz

Clear quartz crystal containing thin threads (called "rutiles") of gold, titanium, or asbestos, which are called "Venus hair" or "Thetis hair," which augment the transmission power of the quartz. Associated with Gemini and Taurus, it enhances life energy, increases clairvoyance, transmutes destructive energy, aids in communication with one's higher self, and increases the efficacy of magic generally.

Tourmalinated Quartz

Clear quartz with inclusions of black tourmaline, which is attuned to Libra. It balances all extremes and is a powerful grounding and protective stone. Absorbs destructive energies, especially feelings of loss and other traumatic emotions. It is a good choice for a grief wand (see below) or one for purification.

Serpentine

This green stone with light and dark hues and white or black speckles protects from "snakebite"—being bitten by the search for knowledge and poisoned by self-superiority and pride because of it or becoming obsessed with seeking hidden knowledge. Increases prudence and self-restraint. In a wand it is well-suited to spells of travel, protection, and wisdom.

Wanderings: The Transmutar Wand

A CRYSTAL-TIPPED WAND is known as a transmutar wand, and it is used in association with two other tools that employ a simple form of crystal magic. These other tools are the base crystal or collector and the crystal necklace, which is known as the controller. The collector holds magical energy as a reservoir (so it is usually in the center of the sacred space), the controller draws the energy from the collector and charges the aura of the magician, and the transmutar wand is used to direct the power that is so collected. A transmutar wand can be used to divide and ward areas of sacred space as well as draw lines of force, summon spirits, and even charge objects. The crystal also has the abilities to remember previous workings and can release energy signatures from those other workings on demand. Thus, the crystal wand is able to store considerably large volumes of magical energy and be able to recall them simply because a many-faceted crystal has within it many angles and facets where lines of force can reverberate and resonate indefinitely.

—Frater Barrabbas, author of
Mastering the Art of Ritual Magic

Tiger's Eye

A variety of quartz with silky chatoyancy, tiger's eye is usually striped yellow and golden brown. Its beauty conveys the temperament of the tiger. Attuned to the constellation Leo, a powerful protective stone through the inspiration of courage. The stone balances emotions and gives clear insight to free one from fears and anxieties. It grounds and centers the user and thereby also strengthens the will.

Turquoise

Turkish blue, this stone carries the power of copper, sacred to Venus. Sky blue turquoise melds the magical powers of Venus and Jupiter. Also sacred to Hathor, goddess of the Milky Way, Boann, and Brighid, anciently associated with milk. Use in weatherworking; spells of expansion, attraction, and repulsion; and love and prosperity (especially green turquoise).

Inclusions in Wands

Besides attaching crystal points or reservoir stones to a wood wand, you may also wish to include something inside it. This means to enclose it either physically or etherically. The word "inclusions" is used to describe minerals that have some other mineral inside them (for example, tourmalinated quartz described above). In a wand, the inclusion is placed by the wandmaker or the owner of the wand. I do not recommend cutting open a wand; however, etheric inclusions can be placed in the etheric body of the wand without cutting it materially. Alternatively, some branches have a pith that can be removed to make them hollow and any wood can be drilled out at its pommel end for inclusions, which may then be sealed by setting a stone or crystal reservoir over them.

Material Inclusions

Some wands are made hollow by removing a pithy core, others by drilling a hole; or the wand may itself be made out of a metal tube—copper for instance. Some use magnetized iron wires to create two magnetic poles; others are filled with a fluid condenser—that is a material mixture designed to condense etheric fluids, be they yin or yang. A good source on fluid condensers in wands is Franz Bardon's book *Introduction to Hermetics*. Bardon was not a witch and not many witches care for Hermetic magic (which is admittedly a bit obscure), but in this case the author describes the two "opposite" forces of yang and yin as similar, respectively, to electricity and magnetism in their behavior. It is important not to take this to mean we are talking about ordinary electricity or magnetism as defined by material science. But the forces or energies we call yin and yang are two fundamental principles that are intimately related to each other in a similar way, as the material force of magnetism is related to a current of electrons. It might not even be going too far to consider that the yin

Wood, Bone, Metal, Stone

or "dark" energy is in fact a field of force, which the yang or "light" energy is like a current of particles that can be conducted in the way certain materials will conduct electricity. However, they are both considered to be fluids, not in the material physical sense used by physicists but in the etheric sense of the word.

Apart from fluid condensers or magnetic rods, you can find wands that have almost any sort of inclusions tucked inside—crystals, powders, metals, feathers, hair, bodily fluids, etc. All of which can add to the magic of the wand if you understand what they symbolize or represent. Inclusions must be vividly present to you and evoke a strong feeling in you.

If you include, for example, a lock of your own hair in the wand, this can be done with relative ease if the wand has a reservoir stone or crystal on the pommel. Just drill or gouge out a hole big enough for the hair and then cap it with the stone using putty epoxy. Your own hair or other bodily ephemera will bind the wand to you more closely than anything. If you do this, then it is especially important that you not let other people use or handle your wand.

Enchanting the Ephemera of Magical Beasts

Instead of material inclusions, I prefer to enchant a magical core into the wand that is not material. That preserves the wood intact, for one thing; and for another, it astrally introduces the character of an animal, which adds the influence of the animal kingdom to that of the vegetable and the mineral. You cannot include material phoenix feathers or unicorn hair into a wooden wand, because they are astral creatures. Gryphons, dragons, hippogriffs, hippocampi, and such heraldic beasts in the medieval bestiaries weren't spotted running about physically on the plane of matter. They were spotted by people with the Sight who could see into the astral plane. That does not mean they aren't "real." But it does mean that you are going to have to walk through the portal in your head and go to the astral plane to procure your feathers, hair, scales, and whatnot.

As I explained in *Wandlore*, I do not agree with the idea portrayed in the Harry Potter novels of using dragon "heartstrings." These are the sinews of the heart of a dragon, and however magical they might be, you cannot avoid killing a dragon to get them. Shards of dragon scale are what I recommend. When the dragon sheds his or her scales, they become brittle and will often break into pieces as they tumble down the mountainside from the beastie's nest. Hippocampus scales are much harder to come by, but fortunately hippocampi have manes, so you can find their hair. In fact, you probably have seen shed hippocampus hair on beaches if you've ever been to the seaside. It looks a lot like seaweed.

Of course, you do not need gobs of whatever bodily ephemera you are using. You only need a tiny bit to enchant into the wand. You have to handle and manipulate the ephemera through the astral plane into the astral body of the wand itself. Don't take the process lightly. If you are clumsy you might end up with it stuck inside your own astral body, and believe me, there is nothing more painful than having a unicorn hair stuck in your third eye—except perhaps a shard of dragon scale.

The power of any astral animal is related to its heraldic meaning in most cases, so that's where studying heraldry can come in handy for witches. In some cases the animal is like one on the earth plane. For example, the feather of a spirit owl, the shed skin of a spirit snake, or the hair of a spirit wolf. Ornithologists will tell you that owls are not terribly smart. They just look wise. Spirit owls, on the other hand, are very wise and very magical. Spirit wolves, like most of these, are wild animals and you should remember that. You will need to get to their nest or den to find hair. Unless your personal or tribal totem is a wolf, you are not going to be able to walk right up and say, "Hello, Mr. Wolf, can I have some of your fur?" The most common reason for including the bodily ephemera of astral creatures is because you have some affinity with them.

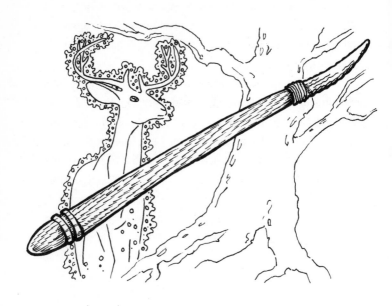

*Embedding an antler point
in a Mabon wand*

Antler Points

One instance where the bodily ephemera of material animals can be used with nicety is cutting the tips off of shed deer antlers with a saw, and using them as wand points. The deer is a sacred animal in many traditions, often figuring in Celtic legends as the creature who appears and disappears mysteriously in the forest, leading the adventurer into its magical darkness. A psychopomp, or guide of souls, the deer (hart or stag) leads into the metaphorical Forest Savage that contains portals into otherworlds. To use antler, I find it looks best if, after imbedding it with adhesive, it is wound with animal sinew or leather to hold it in place. Hide glue or epoxy may be used to secure the point.

Wood, Bone, Metal, Stone

How to Make
a Witch's Wand

𝖀𝖔𝖚 𝖒𝖆𝖞 have one wand or many. One is certainly enough, but some witches like to craft wands for special purposes. A wand can, for example be consecrated to an element other than fire to make it more attuned to spells of information or protection, or for healing or walking the planes and pathways of otherworlds. In chapter 9 I will give you some ideas of special wands you could make. Here we will look at a basic method for making a wand.

Whatever else your wand may resonate with, the most important thing is that your wand resonate with you and that can be best achieved when you make it yourself, pouring your creative energy into it. You will know when a wand is right for you. You will feel an intuitive affinity towards it that feels like it is "calling" you. If you make your own wands, you will be called by a branch and inspired to adapt or decorate it as you

Wanderings: The Ogham Woods

MY PASSION FOR carving wands started as a child of about eight years of age. I loved to carve bits of wood into wands and spears; it felt a very natural thing to be doing. I joined the Order of Bards, Ovates and Druids some twenty or so years ago and one of the lessons suggested that one should attempt to carve a wand out of oak, the druid's tree. Well, that was it. My passion was resurrected and reignited, and since that time I have carved hundreds of wands, mainly in association with the Celtic Irish tree ogham language, the twenty major trees of these islands. So, after oak, I carved silver birch for new beginnings and a yew wand for connecting with the ancestors, ash for the connection with the tree of life and vision questing, and on through all twenty trees.

—Adrian Rooke, Druid (OBOD)

wish (or as it wishes!). Such decoration fits the spirit of the tool to your own spirit.

You can buy wands in shops or commission them made for you by a wandmaker. There is nothing wrong with doing so. However, there is a lot to be said for making your own wand and some traditions require it. Lack of artistic skill is usually the reason to turn to a professional wandmaker who will try to bring what you envision into manifestation. Often a thing of beauty and work of art, such wands can be very inspiring, and it is important to love your wand to create a bond with it.

Buying a Wand

You will find wandmakers with shops online who are catering to magical folk. Many of their wands are made by turning the wood on a lathe, some are sculpted of clay or metals, and some carved or shaped from natural branches. Not all of them are made with magical intention and concentration, enchanted, and given an astral core, but that does not make them any less serviceable. If a wandmaker does approach the making as a mage, then it is good if in his or her enchantment a ritual separate is made from the wand to allow it to bond with you, the owner and user. Yet, there are no hard-and-fast rules in wandmaking any more than there are in other branches of magic—only various traditions and approaches worked out through intuition, inspiration, and thought.

Wandcrafting Yourself

Creation is a divine act. You are employing your inner god and goddess when you create with your own hand and eye. Making your own wand is the best way to create a tool closely molded to your own spirit. What follows are some general tips and guidelines. For a much fuller set of instructions with illustrations, see my book *Wandlore*.

Choosing a Branch and Cutting It

Choosing a branch is the first step. I recommend choosing one from a tree with which you have some familiarity. One on your own property or in your neighborhood is best because it already has an inkling who you are. Picking the tree by affinity and attraction might be better than rationally figuring out you want a wand of elm and then hunting around for an elm tree. A young tree will sometimes be a better choice than an old one because you can more easily reach its branches.

Although cutting a branch from a tree for purposes of making a magic wand is not forbidden, you do have to talk to the tree and ask its permission first, and leave the tree in a healthy state without it being disfigured. Treat this exactly like asking a friend for one of their fingers. I have found that it is best to wait until a tree drops a suitable branch naturally, or until the tree requires pruning for its health or the health of its neighbors. In such cases, you do not get to pick the exact branch for your wand, but you do have the advantage of it being a tree-gift to you, which is, in the end, more powerful.

Not every fallen branch is suitable for a wand. It must be sound. If you try to bend it and it breaks or cracks easily, then it is too far gone. But many branches gifted by trees will still have strength in them and still bear a thread of the dryad spirit of the tree. It is not necessary, in my experience, to have a "virgin" branch cut from a tree with one swoop of the sickle or knife at dawn on a waxing moon. However, if you want to do it that way, there is nothing wrong with it, and it will make the wand more special to you and therefore more closely linked to your own powers. Some mages advise cutting a branch during the tree's dormant period in the winter when the sap is not flowing.

The important thing is to ask the tree for permission and explain to it what you are going to do with the wand. Many trees feel honored to supply a branch that will be used for magic. If you want to cut the branch in the winter, thinking you might spare the tree some pain, be sure to arrange the matter in the summer when the tree is wide awake and coherent.

The actual cutting can be done, in theory, with the single stroke of a mighty sword, but I suggest a pruning saw. This will give a clean cut, which can heal cleanly. If you want to "bandage" the wound, cover it in wax. That will prevent

How to Make a Witch's Wand

insects getting in the wound while it heals up. The wound, if you have cut close to the trunk of the tree or the base of a larger branch, will leave a knot in the wood eventually. That's what knots in wood are—the leftover grain pattern of where a branch met the trunk from which it sprang.

Thanking the Tree

Magical law dictates that something be exchanged for the branch you take. This is to make the exchange equal, and to thank the tree. Starting off your wand magic with an expression of gratitude will set its future on the right footing. Starting out with a gesture of superiority and carelessness will likewise set the tone for your future magical work with the wand.

Removing the Bark

Generally, if there is bark on the branch you will want to remove at least part of it. The handle can remain barked in the case of trees that have tough bark, like oak or elm. Some, like cherry or birch, have thin, loose bark that will pucker and peel as the phloem underneath dries and shrinks. In most cases it is better to smooth and polish the heartwood and get rid of the bark and softwood layer underneath it because these are difficult to seal and preserve.

How to Make a Witch's Wand

Rasping and Sanding

A rasp is a tool you might recognize better by the name of "file." It has a pattern of steel teeth in varying sizes that will cut away the wood. It is good for general shaping because it removes the wood (especially the outer pithy under-bark) much more quickly than sandpaper. Once the shape is worked out with a coarse rasp, you can go over it with progressively finer rasps and then switch to coarse sandpaper (maybe 80-grit) and work your way down to finer and finer grits.

I use 150, 225, and 400 grit, and then a plastic sanding pad equivalent to steel wool. The plastic is a godsend to wand-makers, because steel wool can leave tiny strands of steel in the wood, and iron is the last thing you usually want in your wand unless it is going to be used for scaring away every astral creature in the neighborhood. They won't like you much.

Be Careful with Dust

When sanding, it is wise to wear a respirator or a mask or filter over your mouth and nose to keep out the dust. Safety goggles are also a good precaution to keep the dust out of your eyes. In some wood, the sawdust is actually toxic, but in most cases it will be a matter of protecting your own lungs and mucus membranes. You may also want to wear a smock or apron over your clothes to keep them relatively clean. Protecting your clothes is also important in the next step.

How to Make a Witch's Wand

Wanderings: What's Wrong with Iron?

WHY DO THE Fair folk and the denizens of the "spirit world" flee from iron? An iron-bladed knife is often employed in banishing a circle before work to discourage mischievous entities. The reason is iron's magnetism. When a being manifests on the material plane, the manifestation is usually quite ephemeral. The etheric body that astral beings take on can be disrupted by a magnetic field. Why should they care? Can't they just make a new etheric body? Put yourself in their place: After you have gone to all the trouble to answer a call, give yourself visible form, and make contact, to have someone poke you with an iron rod or blade and disintegrate your etheric body is extremely annoying, not to mention painful.

Wood Finish and Polishing

After getting your wand sanded down smooth and carving it with sigils or whatever you like, you will probably want to stain it. You can leave it white, its natural color, and simply apply an oil finish to it, or you might finish it with shellac, which gives a beautiful sheen but is more fragile than oil. It is best to use a penetrating oil finish such as you can easily find at a hardware store or a woodworking shop. Boiled linseed oil or Danish oil finish are two good choices.

If you want a darker color and to bring out the pattern of the grain, use wood stain. The stain needs to be applied before your final sanding and smoothing because the process of sanding fills up the microscopic pores in the wood and you want these pores open for the stain to penetrate. Try out different colors on scraps of wood—preferably other branches or twigs from your wand branch—to get the color you want. Cherry is a very dark, reddish stain, and mahogany is dark black-brown; black walnut is blackest. There are oil stains and varnishes colored for oak, maple, and birch—the three most common woods for flooring and furniture. You can also find a "fruitwood" or "pecan" that may be quite light in color.

One of the reasons for staining your wood is to seal it; another is to bring out the pattern of the grain. Wood grain will absorb stain unevenly, with the growth rings alternating in darker and lighter shades. In a wood like birch the grain is subtle; in oak or elm, very pronounced. Choose a wood with a close grain—birch, apple, alder, for instance—if you want to do a lot of carving on the wand; that way, your design will be easier to carve and will show up more clearly against the pattern of the grain.

After staining, use the 400 grit sandpaper and the finer plastic pads (these often come in gray, which is more coarse, and white, which is very fine). The wand can be polished by hand using wax or you can put wax on an electric polishing wheel and buff it up that way if you wish. A glassy, shiny finish, or a matte finish—it is all up to your taste.

Attaching Crystals and Stones

If you wish your wand to incorporate stones and crystals, these should not be affixed until the very end, after all the finishing of the wood is done. You will want to prepare the sockets for them to fit into, and this requires some patience. You can use a drill and then work on the hole with a cutting gauge or v-tool. Don't try to get the hole exactly the shape of the end of the stone you want to set in it, just make it a tad bigger in diameter, the same rough shape (e.g., hexagonal for a hexagonal crystal point) and then half-fill the hole with putty epoxy.

Wanderings: The Standing People

IN MY EXPERIENCE, trees and their spirits are frequently surprised to be addressed by humans because it is so rare. They are aware of us, certainly, because we so often do them damage. But our lives are so short by comparison and our manner of locomotion so alien to the standing people, that they do not always realize we are capable of communication. Trees, after all, are connected to each other root and branch. Even the lone oak standing out in a field far from other trees is interconnected with the grasses, the soil, and all the living creatures dwelling in it.

Hold On a Minute: Adhesives

A liquid five-minute epoxy will work to bond stone to wood, but I prefer a putty epoxy, available in several brands and several colors to match lighter or darker shades of wood stain. The important thing in attaching stones is to create the hole to overlap and contain several millimeters of the stone or crystal so that it will be supported by the wood itself. The hole can then be half-filled with putty epoxy, the stone pressed in until it is seated and then the wand put in a vice pointing the with the stone up, so you can get all around it to check whether the stone is straight and true. You will have five or more minutes before the epoxy starts to set in which to adjust it. Some cleanup may be required to cut away any excess adhesive that has seeped out under the stone. A small craft knife or razor blade will accomplish this easily. I use a magnifying glass or jewelers loupe when cleaning up the edges.

Anointing Oils

Besides finishing oils, you can also anoint your wand with ceremonial or magical oils. The making of magical oils and tinctures is a large part of the art of Witchcraft. It is a most practical delivery method for spells. In this case an oil that evokes the fiery element is appropriate (or another element if you are deliberately making a wand of water or wand of air for particular purposes). I anoint my wands with the Water of the Moon and the Oil of the Sun, as follows.

Oil of the Sun

Mix into 8 ounces of almond oil:

      6 drops oil of frankincense

      6 drops oil of orange

      6 drops oil of cinnamon

Mix well.

Consecrate the mixture with this incantation:

> *Power of the sun,*
> *The source of growth and life,*
> *I consecrate this oil to thee.*
> *O supernal Light*
> *Let all touched by this oil*
> *grow and prosper.*

Place it in a clear vessel in the bright sunlight for six days beginning at noon on a Sunday when the sun is in a fire sign (Aries, Leo, or Sagittarius). Depending on where you live, you will probably find Leo to be the best chance of getting six sunny days in a row. Alternatively it may be made at or just before Midsummer's Day, when the sun is at its greatest strength.

Water of the Moon

The moon has natural affinities with elemental water because of her influence on the oceans' tides. Water and the moon both carry the power of the Divine Feminine. You will want to use pure spring water for this purpose, or at least filtered water. If you can get water from a sacred spring, so much the better. Add to the water three pinches of sea salt. You can find sea salt from the Isle of Anglesey in Wales, which is an ancient and sacred Druidic island full of the spirits of our ancestors and the heroes of British legend. I found this salt in a gourmet shop.

Set the bottle of saltwater in the light of the full moon for three nights (include the night before and after the night that the moon is technically at full). It is best if the nights are clear and the bottle is set outdoors in the moonlight. It is best of all when the full moon rides high in the sky.

After it has absorbed the light for three nights cast a circle as indicated above (or according to your own tradition) and, once done, hold your palms open toward the bottle of water. Enchant it with the following triple blessing or something similar:

Waters of the moon,
Be blessed with the light of Arianrhod,
the silver wheel!

Be blessed with the power of Llyr,
the deep lord of the seas!
Be blessed with the joy of Dylan, son of the wave!
I consecrate you for the Great Work.
If it harm none, so mote it be!

I use the names of Welsh divinities in this example. You may substitute any other suitably water-related deities, angels, saints, etc. The important thing is that these aspects relate to water in nature, to the emotions, which are the astral part of the element, and to the moon. Do not get hung up on whether they are of the male or female sex. If you want to evoke only a moon goddess or if you want to invoke only a sun goddess, that is just fine.

The Water of the Moon and Oil of the Sun may be used to anoint people, objects, or candles, as well as wands. Just don't get the sun oil in your eye by accident and do not take either of them internally! Other planetary oils can be purchased or created for anointing wands. Incenses dedicated to particular planets or elemental forces can also be employed. I tend to stick to Nag Champa, but it is entirely a matter of taste and how far you wish to go in getting correspondences just so. You can enhance the experience of wand enchantment by draping your altar with an indigo cloth. When enchanting Water of the Moon, you may drape it in a white or silver cloth.

How to Make a Witch's Wand

Enchanting Your Wand

To begin your quest inward and upward within your consciousness, you first must attach yourself to your wand. If it is a wand that has been enchanted to awaken the dryad of the tree it was made from, then you at once have an intelligent ally. The spirit of the wand, however conceived, makes it a living thing, not merely a poking stick. If you make your wand with the bodily ephemera of astral creatures like unicorns, gryphons, and phoenixes, then it will take on some of the properties of those entities too.

If the wand contains a crystal or stone reservoir, or a mineral point, these also have spirits, and such intelligences are capable of assimilating our thoughts and understanding them in their own way. Trees think very slowly and on a rhythm much more slow than our brainwaves—stones, even more slowly. Thus, it is part of the meditation practice of communicating with your wand to lower your own brainwaves down into the theta and delta range, deep, slow, and deliberate.

What follows is the ritual I use, along with its accompanying gestures to enchant a wand. You will easily perceive how to adapt it to your own wand and its components.

Preparation

Prepare yourself for magical work. Bathe in a ceremonial bath with herbal oils appropriate to cleansing, robe yourself and retire to a place set aside for the art—a room, a shrine, or an outdoor sacred place.

Seat yourself before an altar arranged with manifestations of the four elements:

- a dagger or athame representing elemental air
- a stone or a pantacle (low dish) of salt representing elemental earth
- a cup or bowl, representing elemental water (filled with Water of the Moon)

The element of fire is represented by your wand. However, also place a censor of lighted incense in the south, directly before you, to represent this element. On the altar also have:

- a bell
- a bottle of Oil of the Sun
- your book of shadows
- a large beeswax pillar candle in the center (lit)

Set the wand you are going to enchant on the altar in front of you as you face north.[3] When you are ready, fall into meditation to get into the proper state of consciousness.

---

3 North has been the direction from which magic comes in Celtic and much northern European mythology—it is the place of darkness, mystery, the womb of night. Adapt according to your own tradition as always.

Casting the Magic Circle

Using your hand, a staff, or another wand, circle three times, intoning three times:

> *I cast this circle round me now*
> *And with protective force endow,*
> *With ethereal flame sublime,*
> *Marking sacred space and time*

Take particular care to invite the good spirits of the elements to aid your work of enchantment. In my practice this takes the following form:

Face east and say:

> *In the name of the Hawk of Dawn soaring in the*
> *clear, pure air, I call upon you, O Spirits of the East*
> *and the element of air. Send unto me your ministering*
> *sylphs to aid me in this work. Grant me your wisdom,*
> *your protection, and your strength. Welcome!*

Cross arms over breast, with each hand touching the opposite shoulder, bow and say:

> *So mote it be.*

Face south and say:

*In the name of the Stag of Summer in the heat of the
chase, I call upon you, O Spirits of the South and
the element of fire. Send unto me your ministering
salamanders to aid me in this work. Grant me your
wisdom, your protection, and your strength. Welcome!*

Cross arms over breast and bow as before, then say:

So mote it be.

Face west and say:

*In the name of the Salmon of Wisdom in the
deep, clear waters of the pool, I call upon you,
O Spirits of the West and the element of water.
Send unto me your ministering undines to aid
me in this work. Grant me your wisdom, your
protection, and your strength. Welcome!*

Cross arms over breast and bow as before, then say:

So mote it be.

Face north and say:

*In the name of the Starry Bear of the winter sky,
I call upon you, O Spirits of the North and the element
of earth. Send unto me your ministering gnomes to*

How to Make a Witch's Wand

aid me in this work. Grant unto me your wisdom,
your protection, and your strength. Welcome!

Cross arms over breast and bow as before, then say:

So mote it be.

Face center of circle[4] and say:

Welcome, blessed spirits, to this circle of
work. Keep off all malevolent forces and
banish all disturbing thoughts.

Ring a bell and bow one last time toward the center.

Consecrating and Anointing the Wand

Sit before the altar facing north. Take up the wand you are
going to enchant in your right hand and hold it over the candle
flame. Move it back and forth gently without putting it
into the flame directly. Say:

Wand of oak (or whatever wood it is),
I consecrate you with the secret fire…

Wave the wand in the smoke of your incense, saying:

---

4   In my case, I am standing with my feet on the east side of
center, facing the center, my altar located north of center.
When I sit, I am at center. In a larger circle of art, I have a fire
pit at the center, so I sit outside of that before my altar, which
in that place is situated in the east.

How to Make a Witch's Wand

With the clear intelligence of air…

Hold it against your altar stone or pantacle of salt, saying:

With the manifesting power of earth.

Anointing with Water of the Moon and Oil of the Sun

Dip your finger into the Water of the Moon you have on the altar and stroke the water over the length of the wand, saying:

I anoint you with the lustral waters of the moon…

Uncork your bottle of Oil of the Sun and using your finger again run a small drop of oil along the shaft of the wand, saying:

…and the Oil of the Sun.

Giving the Breath of Life

Put the reservoir end of the wand to your lips, breathe on it gently and whisper:

I breath into you the breath of life. Awaken!

With your breath, envision the core of the wand glowing with light as a hot ember would glow if you blew upon it.

Introducing the Core

(This step is optional and you may be guided by your preference. If it seems powerful, do it. If it seems silly, definitely do not. You will need to have traveled in the astral plane before this ceremony, and procured the core material, whatever it is.)

Still holding the wand in both hands with the reservoir end to your lips, breathe on it a second time and visualize the core material you wish to enchant into the wand as a luminous strand of light that glows brighter when you breathe on it.

Say:

> *I enchant into you a core of phoenix*
> *feather (or whatever the core is).*

At this point, your concentration must bridge the worlds, taking from the astral plane the phoenix feather, unicorn hair, etc., and moving it ethereally in the plane of its existence into the astral dimension of the wand in your hand. This is another bit that is hard to explain, and cannot be demonstrated in the normal sense. You will have to experiment and practice until you can feel and visualize this happening.

Charging the Wand with Sound

If you have a wand you are using to perform the enchantment, touch its tip to the pommel or reservoir stone of the wand being enchanted, tap it three times, visualizing the etheric energy flowing through your hand and wand into the new wand. As you tap it, say:

Magnum Mysterium. Omnium Magicum Est.[5]

Next, place the wand between your hands with the tip in the center of your left palm and the reservoir or pommel of the wand in the center of your right palm. Chant *Awen* or *Oum* to focus your attention into your own light-body and then create a current of prana between your palms, passing through the wand, charging it with life and light. The palm points are called lao gong points by Taoist wizards and masters of qigong.

Sealing the Enchantment and Receiving the Name

After you have chanted long enough to feel that the wand is charged and aware, take it again in your right hand and lift it over the candle flame, declaring:

> *The Maker of Trees has made you*
> *a branch of oak (or whatever it is).*
> *I, (your magical name), have made*
> *you a wand of magic.*

---

5   This is not grammatical Latin. It is a magical form of Latin, which uses endings not according to grammatical rules but for the magical effect of their sound alone. There is no tense or case, time or place in magical incantations. They simply are, timelessly.

Now, touch the side of the wand to your brow chakra (or third eye) and ask politely:

> *Spirit of this wand, if it be thy will,*
> *reveal unto me thy secret name.*

Listen. If the spirit wishes it, you will hear in your mind's ear a whispered name. In my experience, this name can take any form, coming from various magical traditions, languages, or it may be simply a strange and mysterious name. This takes some careful listening. Once you hear the name say:

> *(Name), thou shalt be called. (Name), go*
> *well, do good work, harm no one.*

Kiss the wand in greeting and affection and set it aside to your left, or back upon the altar with your left hand. The kiss is a sign of affection and intimacy and an acknowledgment that the wand is now a living being with a life of its own. So is the use of the familiar "thou" form in English.

Closing and Grounding

Close the circle as you customarily do, according to your tradition, thanking the spirits who have aided you in the Work. At the end, ground yourself by touching the earth or floor of your sanctum and deliberately feel any excess accumulation of magical power go into the earth. Eating a snack is also grounding (chocolate is recommended).

Wand Dedication

A ceremony of dedication may be done after the wand has been enchanted and charged, especially if the wand you are dedicating comes to you as a gift or is made by someone else's hands. The purpose of dedication is to bond your wand to you and to solemnly state your intention with regard to how you will use the wand. In form it is similar to the ceremony of enchantment. Essentially, however, the enchantment is a birthing spell of creation, while the ritual of dedication is a binding spell. It may also be adapted to initiate a wand for a special purpose, color, or type of magic.

Preparation

On a Sunday, in the hour of the sun, on a night when the moon is full or waxing, and (ideally) both moon and sun are in a fire sign, prepare an altar indoors or outdoors with symbols of the four alchemical elements placed in each of the four cardinal directions according to the correspondences.

Creating Sacred Space

Cast a circle in the manner you usually do. Call the quarters and invite the spirits of the four elements to bless your ceremony. Once the altar and space are ready, you may proceed with the work.

How to Make a Witch's Wand

Consecration of the Wand

Sit on the south side of your altar with the candle in front of you, as you face north. Hold the wand in both hands at the level of your heart.

Ground and center your energies by meditating and focusing on the candle, then onto the wand. Raise the wand over the candle flame with your right hand and say:

Wand of magic, I consecrate you with the sacred fire.

Hold the wand so that its point is in the center of your left palm and its pommel or reservoir stone in the center of your right palm. Intone the mantra *Awen* (pronounced Ahh-hh-OOOOOO-ennnnnn), or other magic words, repeatedly while dropping into trance. The syllables should be vibrated in the throat. This way of intoning is common among magical traditions and is less like singing than it is like Tibetan "throat singing" in which overtones and undertones may vibrate with the main tonality.

Feel your prana flowing through your palms and through the wand from right to left. See, in your inner eye, the wand glowing with inward light, its core scintillating with its particular colors, spiraling from the handle of the wand to its point and out into your left hand. Feel this current of power, this current of magical force running through the wand and your body. Visualize the flow increasing in speed and intensity.

Dedicating the Wand

Hold the wand over the candle flame (but not in it) and say:

I dedicate you, (name), to the art of magic, to
goodness, and to the direction of my will.

Say the wand's secret name when you address it this way. Then say:

Join with me and serve no other, in
love, trust, and companionship.

Then kiss the wand and rest with it in your lap for some time, listening to the dryad spirit of the wand. If it speaks to you, engage it in conversation.

Closing and Grounding

When you are finished, close your ritual circle in your usual way. Ground yourself by eating and drinking something to celebrate.

Following the dedication ceremony, spend as much time in physical contact with your wand as you can for several days. Sleep with it under your pillow or, if you are a restless sleeper, somewhere safe nearby. Keep it within the immediate proximity of your aura for seven days. Or, if you wish, for one full month, or for nine months—all good mystical time periods.

How to Make a Witch's Wand

Wand Gestures
and Geometry

Rather like good form in golf, the point of using a wand at all, rather than just your finger or your eyes, is mainly to direct your magical intention more forcibly. You could golf without clubs, but you would not drive the ball so far or so accurately.

Once you have prepared all the other elements of your spell—colored candles, herbs, incense, some object to represent the recipient of the spell, determined the proper astrological timing, and checked the auspices—you will usually intone or chant an incantation that sums it all up in a rhyme. There are many other books that can give you the basic method of constructing spells (see, for example, Illes and Cunningham in the bibliography). Study poetry before writing your incantations. They work better magically if the meter and rhyme scan well.

How you move your wand will depend upon the purpose of the spell. The whole spell is a symbolic structure that you are building up to contain magical forces—the power of your imagination and spirit. In many acts of the magical arts, you will be directing cosmic forces. In other words, the "energy" doesn't come out of your being, but your being acts as a channel through which the force—or etheric fluid—is directed.[6] Your highly polished intention is the lens through which that astral light is beamed, and if it is foggy or smudged, the beam might go astray or fail in its purpose. The thing about magic is that, like a laser beam, it will probably have *some* effect, even if it isn't the one you intended. Remember, never point it at a mirror, either literal or metaphorical. You could put an eye out.

A wand is most often used in a gesture of pointing, to project magic in a specific direction. If you want peace in the Middle East, cast your spell in that direction. But if you want to affect a particular person, you might point your wand in the direction of that person, or you might point it at an object or photograph on your altar, which represents that person. When the wand is pointed in this way, the actual magical process going on inside your mind, body, and spirit are invisible

---

6 That's right and not right at the same time. Your Being (capital B) contains all cosmic forces, but I am assuming you are not yet at the point where you can feel that or slip your consciousness into the archangelic plane.

Wand Gestures and Geometry

to the ordinary eye and indescribable in ordinary language. Moreover, different mages will experience the thing differently. When I point my wand, there is a very particular focusing of my attention, my eyes, ears, and other senses, toward the object of my spell. If I'm doing it right, I will feel my etheric energy being directed through the wand, and my intention focusing it. Everything else will momentarily fade out of existence.

It is tempting to say that one "imagines" one's energy flowing through the wand, but it isn't quite so much imagining as it is just seeing it happen and not thinking about it. There is an element of visualization, but there is a difference between conjuring the image or vision of light and just letting it flow through you. Again, I will make the analogy to correct form in golf or tennis. You don't arrive there by thinking about it, but through training your mind and body to move in the desired way. Moving astral light means training your etheric and astral bodies in a similar manner. If you feel your spell sailing away in a beautiful line toward the goal, that is what counts. And then all the magic pros can sit around the nineteenth hole with a Scotch and soda and argue about what is really "correct" form.

In the case of sports, the muscles have their own sort of memory in the part of the brain called the cerebellum. In magical work, one uses other parts of the brain, parts that are deep, primordial, and mysterious. In anatomical maps, these regions of the brain are marked "Here Be Dragons." In the old days, it was called working from the heart. Or the liver. (The pineal gland?) The latest medical opinion seems to be that the brain's temporal lobes might do the trick.

Similarly, you must become one with your wand, moving it not in a single "correct" form but intuitively in the correct form for the work you are performing. It is really more like the gesture of an actor than the "form" of an athlete. On the other hand, I think that the true athlete goes beyond rationalized forms into the intuitive.

Tapping is a tried-and-true method of transferring power through a wand. In the old Irish and Welsh legends of Druids and denizens of Fairyland, a tap on the head was all that was needed to turn a prince into a pig. If you have the object of your spell right in front of you, a tap may be more appropriate than waving. It may also be appropriate to draw a rune or sigil on the object.

Finally, in some actions, prolonged contact between the wand and the object of enchantment is useful. For example, in wand enchantment itself, contact may be maintained between the point of the wand doing the magic and the reservoir of the wand receiving it.

The proper form for
wand enchantment

The same technique may be applied to charging talismans or balancing chakras or to healing in general. Here again it is the contact between the etheric bodies of the wand and the object of healing that counts. The creation of the two points of a line inherently creates "contact," but to, as it were, bring those points together through touch is most effective.

Wands are used to invoke or evoke spirits and deities. In such cases, simply hold the wand upright in front of you or with your hands across your chest if you approach with that humble posture. Do not point at gods; it's not polite. Pointing a wand at mischievous spirits is appropriate because you are commanding them. Other beings such as faerie folk and nature spirits will only be startled if you point at them. They do not need to be commanded. You need to get to know them first and then ask for their help.

A wand is pointed outward and downward to cast a magic circle, or straight out to draw pentagrams in banishing rituals. This inscribing in the air may be used for writing runes or other signs also. A wand is often used to astrally stir potions and to charge them with intention. It may move over the surface of the potion or point straight down into it to imbue it. Likewise, it may swirl the astral energies of a bowl of water for scrying, or bless a goblet of mead.

Wand Gestures and Geometry

Crossed posture for holding a wand

In the end, the wand works by motion and direction. It's shape and structure assist in the movement of ethereal forces because you can relate at a deep level of your brain to the movement of your body. The gesture of the wand is a ritual movement and, after practice, becomes a key to unlocking the inner depths of the mind. Those depths are the doorways to the higher realms, and within those higher dimensions of existence the gesture of pointing or creating a swirling vortex of power becomes an irrevocable force—a force indeed that changes what happens in the world below.

Stirring a vortex above a cauldron

Drawing Shapes and Sigils

The most common use for your magic wand will be in casting circles. The most basic of magical techniques, nearly all traditions use circles as a geometric figure traced either literally on the ground in chalk or other substance, on a ground cloth, or drawn astrally with a wand, sword, or athame. A circle with a point at its center, or a circle crossed from top to bottom and left to right are each symbols of the sun. Other planetary glyphs are compounded of circle, crescent, and cross.

In the Lesser Banishing Ritual of the Pentagram, the pentagram symbolizes the five senses of the human body and also the five elements of alchemy, including the quintessence, which is represented by the point at the top of the "star." Banishing pentagrams are drawn from different starting points depending on various factors. One might wish, for example, to make a banishing pentagram of earth by starting with the lower left corner and sweeping upwards. The wand can be used to draw any symbolic shape.

Circles

Drawing—or, as we say, "casting"—a circle uses the geometric figure that symbolizes oneness, closure, wholeness, and finiteness. It encloses working space and sets a boundary to the timeless, eternal realm you create for magical work. Doing magic without enclosing yourself in a circle is like trying to paint a picture on a moving city bus. It is possible, but not really the ideal place. As a painter has her studio, the witch has her circle.

Drawing a circle with a wand, whether around yourself or around something else isolates it and by analogy protects it. Unlike a polygon, a circle has no points, no corners, no weak spots. It does not represent the joining of several powers: It represents the union of all things. Yet, paradoxically, it isolates one thing at its center from everything else outside its circumference.

For Pagans the circle is usually thought of as sacred space, enclosing and protecting one's work in the astral realm. When a circle is cast with a wand, your will is projected into it, to sustain its reality for a limited time. The mind is used to imagine it; the will to believe it into manifestation. It is erected temporally but contains a zone of no-time.

Circles are cast to the right (sunwise) to set them into sync with the sun's apparent motion. Sun and moon and stars all rise and set from east to west with Earth's rotation. Clockwise is defined according to the direction of the planet's rotation and the apparent movement of the sun. So, the action of the wand links the circle to Earth, which is itself sacred. When you rotate with your wand and imagine a circle of blue light around your sacred space, sweep it overhead as well to create a dome, and extend the arc below your feet to make a complete sphere.

Once your circle is cast, you will go about your business within it, and in those actions also you will be drawing shapes with your wand. Even if it is merely held still pointing up, down, right, or left, forward, or back, your wand participates in the geometry of the six directions and makes straight lines of an infinite extension. Your hand holds that infinite extension of will and imagination, and links the six outward directions with the seventh: inward. That is, the direction of your inner depths.

It is the exploration of this inward dimension that is the first work of the initiate, no matter what tradition he or she may follow. The circle is the place for any action appropriate to the idea of the sacred—that is, something set apart from ordinary reality. Sacred implies holiness, which implies wholeness, and the wholeness implied is related to the number one and to infinity. It unites. At the highest level, it unites the very ideas of unity and diversity and leads to cosmic consciousness—or as you may prefer, oneness with nature or the Divine.

When you are ready to close the work, you close the circle by doing everything you did to open it, only in reverse order. This alludes to the directions forward and backward, and again to the structuring of all action, all time and motion, according to the analogy of the sun's apparent movement.

Triangles

I like to draw my circles three times round and unwind them three times back, which ties my motions also to the number three. Three is, of course, the number of points in a triangle. Such a three-pointed structure is the first polygon, the first closed shape possible with the least number of lines—signifying primordial closure or enclosure. Three wands may form a triangle. Three sweeps of one wand likewise may form a triangle. To what does the triangle allude? To the union of opposites. While the line (formed of two points connected) alludes to the connection of two things (for example, the witch and the object of her will), the triangle takes all pairs and unites them in a synthesis of their qualities.

This can take many forms, of course. It happens when three ingredients are mixed in a spell, potion, or concoction. It happens when man and woman, Masculine and Feminine are united in a third reality: a couple, as we say, which is not "two" as the word "couple" usually suggests, but a "marriage" in the general sense of that word; a melding of two individuals into one that is capable of much more than either part by itself. The couple also produces another kind of "third thing"—a child, which then becomes a completely separate and unique individual, ready to achieve union with another.

The triangle symbolizes Divinity. This should provide a clue to what we mean by the Divine: Not merely "ecstasy" (extending beyond oneself) but the result of that ecstasy, which is a new union and a new oneness as its "offspring." The magic wand of the witch or wizard represents the linear two and their union, thus it also holds within its mystery the triangle: the three-in-one, and the one made of the connection between one and two. To use another mathematical metaphor, the wand represents addition; it embodies the joining of two points, the creation of connection that produces a combination of the two things.

Squares

Squares are used alone and also in conjunction with a circle. For example, the four cardinal directions form a square and invoking them is sometimes called "squaring the circle." This embodies an ancient secret of the stonemasons: how to use a circle and two parallel lines to draw a perfect right angle of ninety degrees. This angle has been crucial for the construction of sound buildings—to make sure they are straight and upright, 90 degrees in relation to Earth's gravity. You might say, *well, what does squaring an angle have to do with magic?* Anciently, the mathematics and geometry used to determine a right angle were considered magical. It was a way to control one of the invisible forces of nature (gravity) to create balance and harmony, using a ritual process.

The square magically embodies the number four, which is the number of Earth. When our ancestors thought the world to be a square, they were idealizing what they saw: a flat surface, or plane. The idea of the "four corners of the world" came from this idealization.

If a structure's building blocks and columns were "square," and plumb, it would endure. If it was square it was true. Thus the square becomes a symbol for truth; its equal sides and angles become a symbol of equality. So, equality and truth are seen to be intimately related—a kind of perfection, not only of architecture but of society. By extension, this kind of perfection is equally desirable in magic.

The square is metaphorical in magic, but the trueness of a spell, the "balancing" of its parts into an equal relationship is crucial to success. The four points of a square symbolize Earth, our planet, our whole world; however, they also symbolize the four elements as the component parts of that world. Earth, air, fire, and water must be precisely balanced

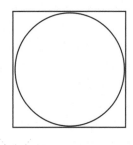

The circle squared

Wand Gestures and Geometry

and equal to underly the wand's use to create a balanced intention. With a harmony among these four elements, the spell and its results will be enduring and resist the forces that try to tear it down.

The Point and Line

As suggested earlier, the most fundamental action of a magic wand is to define two points—an origin and an end—and then join them with a line. The wand is the line, you are the origin, and the object of your art is the other point with which you are establishing a relationship. In a lot of magic, the relationship is intended to be temporary, but like all relationships, magical relationships are sticky. They persist. Even if you forget about them temporarily they can pop up again in the most startling ways. This is why the relationship or connection between the two metaphysical points in a spell have to be undone. The spell that creates the bond has to be ritually undone to break the connection and has to be something both parties agree to wholeheartedly.

To "draw" a point with a wand is a simple tap or pointing gesture, and can be used to manifest intention to identify something as an object of magic. The action can never be done without implying a line; however, as you and your hand holding the wand are always the point from which the object is located, you are the center of the circle.

161

The point within the circle

You are at a center and cast an effect outward to a specified distance and direction, so that the second point (the object of your spell) may be imagined to be on the circumference. Alternatively (or at the same time) you can imagine the object as a point within another circle describing how the effect upon it will influence things surrounding it. This is a good image to draw with a wand and your imagination for spells of circumstance, or when you wish to influence the circumstances surrounding a person or object (e.g., a protection spell, a wealth-attracting spell, a blessing).

Runes and Sigils

From the basic shapes, Witchcraft moves on to the drawing of runes (which may be the letters of the Norse Futhark or other magical alphabets and signaries), each of which is designed to carry certain energies. For example, in a finding spell I employ the rune Fehu from the Norse system because it represents portable property or possessions, and when I am looking for something I have lost (pens and keys usually) this rune taps into the cosmic category, so to speak, and brings its power to bear on returning my property.

In wandwork it is usually best to use such runes or sigils—designs made up of a number of letters combined—instead of writing out long sentences or whole words. The thought is made more powerful by being made compact. A sigil can be drawn using combinations of symbols—such as the astrological symbols for planets and signs, etc.—or it can be a merging of the initial letters of a sentence that states your intention. The result is a figure that can be drawn with the wand as well as with ink upon a talisman. (See Pennick on magical alphabets and Cooper on sigils.)

Raven Grimassi, in his book *Hereditary Witchcraft*, illustrates some witch signs that convey such general powers as protection or manifestation. These can be drawn with a wand in addition to pen and ink, or can be carved into the shaft of a wand to reinforce its special purpose.

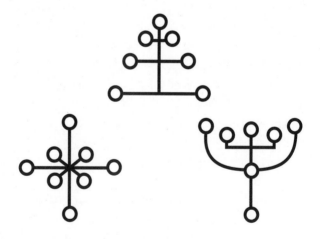

Witch signs for manifestation (top), protection (bottom left), and transformation (bottom right)

Wanderings: Rune Magic with a Wand

ONE WAY THAT I like to use a wand is to draw the power of a rune into my energy field. Let's suppose I am doing something basic like prosperity magick. I will ground and center within a cast circle, then create images of prosperity before me: perhaps a nice new home, or a bankbook with a hefty balance in my account, or myself smiling and writing checks to my favorite charities and causes.

When these are vivid in my mind, I will inhale energy from the ambient field, then exhale it and draw the rune Fehu (also called Fe or Feoh, meaning cattle or wealth) before me in the air, glowing brightly and absorbing the energy of my prosperity images. When it reaches a peak of brightness, I inhale deeply, drawing in the glowing rune with my breath. Then I say my standard safeguard, "With harm toward none, and for the greatest good of all, so mote it be!" The spell is complete, except of course that I must now "act in accord" by doing what I can on the material plane to bring prosperity.

—Amber K, author of *True Magick: A Beginner's Guide, CovenCraft: Witchcraft for Three or More*, etc.

The Witch's Wand
in Specific Spells

The following are spells provided to demonstrate the use of the witch's wand in a particular context. These spells are nothing new and are chosen for their value as demonstrations of the various types of magic you might do; that is, spells of information, spells of circumstance, and spells of transformation. (For more on spellcrafting, I recommend Blaxell, Dolnick, and Illes in the bibliography.)

Spell for Protection

Protection spells are a type that shapes the circumstances around the object you wish to protect, preventing accidents or harm. Let's apply it to a car. It does not make your car physically invulnerable; it causes events to flow around it, metaphysically averting harm (and parking tickets if you work it well).

- Get in the proper magical frame of mind.

- From outside your car raise your wand from ground upward, pointing at the left front fender. Visualize a black pillar rising up in front of the left headlight. Take your wand and wave it in a spiraling motion parallel to the ground to help indicate how the pillar rises up, for it is a pillar of energy and intention. Wait until you see the pillar very clearly in your mind's eye.

- Once you have that, keep it going in your mind and envision a white pillar rising in front of your right headlight. This, too, is energy, but it is the inverse of the black energy. The black pillar is yin. The yang energy of the white pillar flows out of it. Move your wand in the same gesture: upward from the ground, again with a spiraling motion.

- Keep the two front pillars going, and with the same gesture of your wand raise up a black pillar at the right taillight. You are alternating the polarity of the force at work so that it will run in a circuit around the four sides of the box you are making.

- Add another white pillar at the left taillight. Keep them all spiraling up from earth to sky, intensifying together.

- Imagine these pillars protecting your car and then let the white energy flow to the black and the black to the white, like polar opposite forces around the perimeter of the box, until you get a box of energy around the car on all sides flowing from these four dynamic pillars.

- Envision a roof to the box around the car, supported by the pillars and flowing out of them. Black and white join together in this solid temple of protection. The wand gesture accompanying this part of the spell is to draw an arc above the car, imagining a dome.

- Finally, after holding that vision for a moment, let a guardian spirit appear. Point your wand where you want to see this guardian, sailing around the car on the stream of energy.

- Do not reject whatever form the guardian spirit takes. If it is a dragon flying around, super. But if it is a polar bear or a pirate ship or a rubber duck, do not respond by saying to yourself, "Oh, that's ridiculous." Just accept whatever form it takes. It is a guardian. It doesn't have any single form in the material world, and what it gives you is probably taken from something in your unconscious mind, which means that it is intimately linked to you.

The Witch's Wand in Specific Spells

Watch the guardian circling for a minute and then welcome it by saluting with your wand raised toward it and ask it to protect your car from harm. (A little rhyme here is nice.)

- You can ask for specific protection (from accidents, from parking tickets, from being stolen) or just generally. I tend to do both: ask for total protection from harm and specific protection from whatever it is that concerns me at the moment.

As with all spells, forget it, trust it, and don't worry about it. Plant the seed and let it work and grow. You can repeat the spell periodically, maybe even each time you get into the car, but as you do so you will trust it more and realize that it won't really lose its charge or momentum so long as you continue to believe in it without interfering constantly. The only way a spell can "wear off" is if the person casting it ceases to keep it in his or her unconscious mind.

When I say "forget it," I do not mean to really forget it. Just don't dwell on it or constantly keep trying to re-cast it because you are not sure it worked. I've done this and had to stop myself. Sometimes a desperate need or fear makes one keep "supplicating" as it were. But you aren't begging for divine intervention, you are casting your will upon the cosmos as a person of power and confidence. That is what the wand signifies.

Potion for Protection

A protection potion embodies the symbolism (and active ingredients, we might say) in a material matrix of herbal essences and alcohol, water, or oil. The purpose of tinctures, potions, and decoctions is to provide a way to save up the power of the various ingredients to manifest what they symbolize. Where the spell gathers together the symbols of protection in the moment, a potion allows the same intention to be bottled. The efficacy of potions is on the astral dimension of a spell of being, just like any other magic. The material vehicle is necessary to link imagination and matter.

So here is a recipe I use for brewing a protection potion. This is not for internal consumption!

- Assemble the following herbs: two bay leaves, five whole cloves, five caraway seeds, powdered garlic (a pinch), blackberry leaves, powdered cumin (a pinch), five fennel seeds, dried rosemary (¼ teaspoon), dried basil (¼ teaspoon).

- Crush all together with mortar and pestle, then, holding your wand over the mixture, chant five times:

Come together to protect against all harm and to effect
A field to repel and avert all harm or defect.

- Fill a small cauldron with water and bring to a boil. Add crushed ingredients and allow to boil for five minutes.

- While the potion boils, draw a pentagram over it constantly with your wand and chant five times:

> *Bubble, bubble, toil and trouble*
> *Fire burn and cauldron bubble.*
> *A shield from harm forever be*
> *To all thee touch or who touch thee.*

- Remove from heat and allow to cool.

- Decant into a clear container, straining through cheesecloth if needed so that the potion is free of large bits or particles from the herbs. It will not be completely clear.

- Combine this mixture with an equal part of pure alcohol or mineral spirits.

- Place the potion in an open vessel on your altar, open your circle and meditate upon it with your wand extended over it. Draw a circle over the vessel slowly and visualize a vortex of steam rising from it, thick and white. Concentrate on the idea of protection, allowing the word to evoke as many images of protection in your mind as you can. When this idea has resolved into a single form in your mind (a metal shield, a guardian angel, or animal, etc.), chant the following closing incantation:

> *By fire's light, by sea and stone,*
> *By rune and sign, by ancient crone*
> *All harm and danger be overthrown*
> *Omnia tangenti protegione.*

- When you say "rune" in the incantation, draw with your wand the rune Eihwaz (᛬), which is a Norse rune for protection. If you wish to devise your own bind rune, do so. When you say "sign" make the sign of a circle and cross—this draws upon the strength of the sun and also represents a round shield.

- The incantation with its rune and signs will be performed to activate the potion each time it is used. If you are applying the potion to a person or object, the rune and sign should be made over that person or object. At the final word, tap the object of the spell with your wand and apply the potion to it. If a person, take a small amount from the bottle with your thumb and apply to the temples and the back of the neck.

If you wish to use this potion to enhance your own ability to cast a protective veil over something, you may apply it to the center of each of your palms, to your own temples and your third eye in the middle of your brow. You may also anoint a wand with this potion to protect it and to empower it to cast spells of protection. The efficacy of the potion, as always, depends as much on your concentration upon the astral dimension of reality as it does on the inherent protective powers of the other ingredients.

To Make Something Invisible

For some reason, invisibility has always been a fascination for witches and magicians. I suppose it is part of the desire for secrecy and protection from prying eyes when engaged in the art. Using invisibility for malicious or mischievous purposes is far more difficult than using it for a benign or neutral purpose. That is because doing something sneaky or wrong runs against the grain of the illusion. This spell again is a manipulation of the circumstances outside of you. You are not transforming your material body into something that cannot be seen; you are changing the way others look at you. You are rendering yourself unnoticeable. Almost everyone has experienced this phenomenon when looking for something, not finding it, and then having it turn up later in plain sight. I usually suspect brownies when this kind of thing happens.

Brownies are the "Borrowers" of tale and legend and things will just disappear and reappear from time to time.

I used to fly into a rage about this, thinking that it defied logic. "I know I put it down right there!!!!" But anger is useless. In such cases, and in all cases of the invisible, what is really going on is a slight shift of the etheric body into the astral plane. One's physical body does not leave the material plane, or "disappear" except in the sense that appearance is perception.

The use of your wand in this kind of spell is to indicate the object you wish to make invisible. To point at it, rather than to draw any shape or rune. You might draw a sigil designed to hold the spell. A sigil is a combination of symbols or letters that you build up to associate with a particular entity or effect. In some old grimoires you will find sigils for angels and demons. These "stand for" the entity as one's signature "stands for" one's assent. Assent means will, and when you draw a sigil, you give your permanent assent to whatever it is you are "signing"—just like a contract.

My spell for invisibility:

- Get into the proper magical frame of mind and body. Hold your wand with the point touching your forehead (or the object you wish to make invisible).

- Visualize yourself (or the object of the spell) fading into transparency and then fading away entirely.

- Recite this incantation:

By sunlight, shadow, and morning mist,
By curlew's call and will-o'-wisp,
I am (or you are) unseen and yet unmissed.
Meum (or Teum) non videus est!

I use a Latin activation phrase at the end of my spells because I find this forces the whole ball of wax into a sort of closure. You should, of course, as ever, end it with "If it harm none, so mote it be." This is a wise precaution because even practiced witches cannot predict all the side effects of their magical reactions.

When performing this spell to make someone else or an object invisible, you will tap your wand on the object or person. Another wand gesture I sometimes use is a sweeping motion from above the object downward, as if drawing down a curtain. As with all such gestures, the key is to visualize and will it as you make the motion.

For Protection of Your House

Spells of home protection often include herbs. Sprinkling crumbled dried basil leaves around the circumference of the foundation is the objective part of one such spell. It can be enhanced by also pointing your wand at the foundations of the house as you walk about it deosil chanting and repeating this incantation:

Protect and preserve the firm foundation of this home
Held fast within this sphere of strongest spelling,
Hestia, goddess of the hearth here come
To keep safe from harm all here dwelling.
Domus defensus ergo sum!

Any spell can be augmented by the addition of the use of herbs, colors, incense, oils and tinctures, candles, and so forth. But often, the simple ways are just as effective, if the will is focused, and the wand wielded well.

You can also perform precisely the same visualization given in the car protection spell to protect your house.

To Draw Blessings to Your Family

For this one you might employ a family photograph or, if your family members are magically inclined, gather them all together.

- Touch your wand three times to the photograph and draw a triangle with your wand. Visualize it in blue light.

- If your family is gathered, touch each in turn on the left shoulder, and then the right, pausing above the head where the Crown Chakra resides. Visualize a triangle thus formed over the head of each family member, which establishes a connection between them and the Highest Realm of the Celestial planes.

- Concentrate upon the blessings you wish to come to your family, whether specific or general. Envision the blessings, don't say it in words until you speak the incantation.

- Repeat this incantation for each:

> *Thus the Lord and Lady showed me,*
> *By a triangle may thy spirit be*
> *connected to the Highest Spirit*
> *By that One who unites us*
> *in the family of Humankind,*
> *Draw down blessings upon you, my*
> *(son, husband, daughter, etc.)*
> *White light within this house dwell willingly*
> *And give us peace. (or, give us*
> *the blessing of _____)*
> *Benedicite omnium familium*

If you are of a Norse persuasion or a practitioner of *seið* (seething), you will know what to do with the Norse runes. These are among the most well-known signs for magical use in our Western culture. In this spell, use your wand to draw the rune Gifu (an **X**) across the heart chakra of each family member or over the photograph.

For Forgiveness and Reconciliation

The great teachers of every age have reminded us of the need for forgiveness and reconciliation. The solution to problems, differences, or arguments is never war. So, before you set out to cast that curse on someone who has wronged you, or allow hate to rise up and dominate your emotional being (the You on the plane of Venus), consider the much safer and ultimately more effective path of forgiveness and reconciliation. As in the previous spell, you may wish to use a photograph of the person against whom you have ill feelings, or write their name upon a parchment slip. Point your wand to this representation and touch it. Then over it draw in green light the astrological symbol for Venus or the Norse rune Wynja thus:

♀   Venus

ᛈ   Wynja (love, joy, hope, friendship)

Recite this incantation:

> *Lord and Lady leading bright through this dark night*
> *Of suffering and anger, conflict and affliction,*
> *Open my heart and the heart of*
> *_____ (whoever it is)*
> *To fill us both with the Love of the Goddess*
> *Source of Love and reconciler of the cosmos.*
> *May anger be dispelled and hurt hurled far from us,*

May friendship and forgiveness
fill the void of the heart's hate.
Fill emptiness with the fair flowers
of fellowship and Light.
Restore the wreck of our relationship
to delight and rest.
Relatio caritatis coniunctionis est!

To Dispel Violence

There could hardly be a more useful spell than this one in our modern world. This spell is not quite the same thing as a protection spell. It is a circumstanciation that aims to avert deliberate violence rather than accidents, and is applicable to the whole world or one's own household. Wherever violence occurs or is threatened it can be dispelled magically. It is not easy, but doing it as a circumstanciation is easier than as a transformation of the heart and mind of the person doing the violence. It is worth noting that the change of heart may come about as a sort of side effect of this spell, but that the spell itself is not aimed at a particular person. It is aimed at the circumstance of violence—what is in the air, so to speak—whether that be personal and close to home or a war and threats of violence perpetrated in a foreign land.

The appropriate sign here is Mars (σ^{7}) and the Norse rune Tyr or Tiwaz (↑). With your wand, draw these signs in blue light (not red, as you would do if invoking them as powers of force or guardianship). Blue symbolizes peace and harmony. The idea here is that you are calling upon the masculine energy of the Lord as guardian and protector, the mature, divine masculine, which does not react out of blind instinct for self-preservation or self-assertion. The symbols may be drawn on something representing the place from which you desire to dispel violence. Or, you may draw the symbols in the air in the direction from which you sense the violence, if it is out in the world. Burning rose incense is appropriate for this spell.

Sing softly the sweetness of strength.
Let the Lord cast forth his ordinance over Earth
That protection come not with violence,
That fear and hate and greed be
dispelled from this place
And the mature Masculine spirit make it secure
And hold the thoughtless child in check.
Cease name-calling; cease provoking;
cease jealousy and hate.
Dispel from this place the fear-framed power
That would strike, lash out, and violate the law of love.

May cooperation in true strength
set itself against violence
Against invasion,
Against domination.
So mote it be.

Such a spell seems especially appropriate for dramatic gestures of your wand—circle it around to take in the whole world. On "dispel" draw a pentagram in the air, and again in each of the final three lines. Draw the pentagram of banishing and point your wand to its center to charge it, visualizing an outward moving force or shield. I would choose an apple wand for this spell, with its love-giving power. Linden, cherry, or ash also are suitable.

For Acquiring Knowledge

An information spell seeks knowledge, wisdom, and understanding. A beech wood wand is especially delightful for this kind of work. Beech has old affinities with books and learning. The wand is, as always, an instrument of fire, but in this case the spell is really one of elemental air, for air is thought, words, and reason, which is how we usually think of knowledge. Spells of information are almost always air spells, and thus a wand of hazelwood is also a good choice. Unless the knowledge you seek is knowledge of feelings and emotions (water), or knowledge of buried treasure (earth), the element of air is likely to dominate.

Beech is a fiery wood but intimately correlated with books. So, if the knowledge is to be found in books, use beech. If not, use hazel. If it is a matter of someone's feelings, use poplar or willow. If it is a matter of seeking wealth or treasure, a wand of elder or elm is advised. In all cases, anointing the knowledge wand with bergamot oil or employing this oil as a scent during the spell will enhance your success. In her *Mama Bear's Musings* blog, aromatherapist and author Mama Bear describes the powers of bergamot thus:

> Bergamot essential oil is a sweet, floral, citrus scent that... lightens the shadows of the mind, bringing joy and laughter to the heart...It can clear away the fogginess that often muddles us, allowing the higher spiritual self to become attuned to our helpers.

It is the quality of unmuddling that is especially helpful, and in cases of seeking higher knowledge, connecting to your spiritual helpers is, naturally, part of the process. Occult or hidden knowledge is almost never a matter of simply reading books or finding old grimoires. One has to work through the higher self to see clearly what is true and exactly how it is true. Otherwise, you might get mere opinion or, worse still, misinformation. It is essential to focus on Truth here—and Truth with a capital T, which means that you should not presume you know what is true beforehand. When seeking information or knowledge, you also need wisdom, which is the ability to suspend judgment until all the facts have been presented and evaluated without bias.

For this spell, trace the symbol of Mercury (☿)in the air. In the tradition of the Celtic bards, the ogham "phagos" for beech can be the seal (ᚺ). If you can find a beech nut, this will go even better. Point your wand at the beech nut, draw upon it the symbol of Mercury (or any appropriate specific symbol or sigil that asks for the particular knowledge you seek), then apply one drop of bergamot oil to the nut. If you cannot procure a nut, use a small piece of serpentine.

You probably have no idea where the knowledge is going to come from when you cast this spell, so if you do not have a beech nut or stone to act as the recipient of the energy, draw the symbols with your wand, facing east, which is the direction of air. Here is the incantation I use:

> *By air and blowing wind,*
> *By all that hides from sight,*
> *Knowledge now unto me send,*
> *With Ogma's wit and owl's flight.*
> *Sapiens Aperi Serpentine!*

Ogma is the Irish lord of communication and language, for whom the oghams are named. You may substitute whatever divine power you prefer as a bringer of wisdom. The owl is traditional and a particular favorite of mine.

Once you have cast the spell, finish off the ritual with a cup of Earl Grey tea, which contains bergamot. Metaphysically "stir" the cup of tea with a deosil movement of your wand before drinking. Carry the nut or stone with you at all times and keep your eyes and ears open.

Knowledge spells can work in many ways. This is why I give them the more general name of "informations" as a type of magic. It may be that rather than acquiring knowledge for yourself, you may want others to gain knowledge of you. Sort of a publicity spell. This can be crucial in any spells for success, but is in fact an Information spell rather than a circumstantiation (manifesting) spell. The same procedures given above can be used for the "know me" spell, except that you employ (in addition to bergamot) a drop of infusion of eyebright. The eyebright herb has the Latin name Euphrasia after the Greek goddess of mirth and joy, Euphrosyne. You can anoint your own eyelids with this infusion when seeking knowledge, anoint your brow when seeking to be known, or anoint the beech nut or serpentine stone, which you can easily leave out of your pocket if fame gets too much for you. For this working the following incantation will do the job:

The Witch's Wand in Specific Spells

Radiant joy and wisdom wild
Make me seem thy perfect child
All shall know my name always
Fame bless me through all my days,
Omnibus Meum Plaudite!

The Wand in Meditation

The first practice of the magical arts is meditation, which simply means to sit still in a disciplined way and manipulate your body's energies. These energies include the body's kinetic energy: keeping still, often in a characteristic posture. It does not need to be an advanced yoga posture. Indeed, if you sit cross-legged on a pillow, or if you lie down, that will be sufficient for most enchantments. This practice should come before one attempts any spellcasting, but your wand can still play a role.

Your energies also include your thoughts, emotions, and dreams. Adding your wand to the practice of meditation gives you something to hold onto and, holding it materially, you can also train yourself to hold it in your astral body on the other planes. Keep your wand in your hand while you are moving your energy (your qi or chi, as the Chinese say). Once you have worked with your wand enough for it to symbolize clearly a connection between your spiritual will and the otherworlds, it can serve as both guide and anchor as you leave your ordinary world and travel astrally.

Having your wand in your hand reminds you that you are able to control what happens. Because it is a magical tool, its power lies within the astral plane, and therefore it is more directly useful when your consciousness is focused there. In that plane, it can be used instantaneously, because the whole plane transcends time. Using your wand through the astral plane to affect the material plane requires that your intention leave the material plane and re-enter it. This means that it will re-enter at a particular time—one that you usually want to predetermine and include in your spell's structure. It might be in the future, or the past. Getting instantaneous response in the present moment is very difficult—comparable to aiming at a number line and hitting a rational number.

There is no question that in the astral worlds one can encounter scary things. In that world ideas are entities. Remember that. Ideas are entities. They may seem like people, or animals, or objects, or monsters, and anything can happen, just as when you are dreaming. This is where you will meet your spirit guides and perhaps your deities. But it is also a world of entities that are overjoyed at the opportunity to lead you astray, lie to you, and dupe you into doing things you know are wrong. One never can assume an astral entity is who he says he is. A beautiful angel may appear and be nothing more than a guise to suck you in and use you. A cute fluffy bunny might appear and then launch itself at your throat.

Fortunately, your wand can help you here. Let it take any shape it wants. You can take any shape you want as well, once you get the hang of it, but try to stay human-shaped for the time being until you are sure you can change back. Pointing your wand at another human being and demanding that he reveal his true identity will most likely result in laughter or a startled expression. Doing the same thing to an astral entity when you are in your astral body will actually work, if you believe it will work. Belief is the key. On the astral plane of existence anything goes, if you believe it into existence. In other words, for the witch, believing (on the astral planes) actually creates whatever is imagined.

Belief is not merely wishing. Our Western scientific culture rejects "wishing" as childish, or as "superstition." The older you get, the more you are taught that "wishing won't make it so" and other such bits of homespun wisdom. The fact is that wishing will make it so, but it is an action that must be serious and truly focus one's imagination to the point of belief. Imagination is not a power to deceive yourself; it is a power to create.

Belief is related to faith in this respect: You have to have faith in your higher self, at least in the moment of doing magic, to be able to achieve belief. Believing something in a

The Witch's Wand in Specific Spells

superstitious way—just because someone else told you it was true—is not what is needed. On the contrary, if you "believe" something to be actually true, that is just knowledge. Believing that your thoughts can manipulate reality is belief through faith, not through trusting authorities. So, in meditation the best work you can do is to get in touch with your higher self—whatever name you wish to give that entity. Believing in your wand is a first step toward that higher realization.

The T'ai Chi Wand

There is a type of t'ai chi (or qigong—which literally means moving chi), that employs a "ruler," a wooden wand about ten inches long with flat ends to fit into your palms. It is intended, in part, to help you learn to keep your hands equidistant when doing some qigong movements. If you look up this method, you will see that some of its techniques can be easily adapted to the use of a witch's wand. Such exercises are very good, both for learning to use your chi and for learning to pass etheric energy through your wand. I recommend *The T'ai Chi Ruler: Chinese Yoga for Health and Longevity* by Terry Dunn. Realize that when Taoists speak in terms of health and longevity, they mean spiritual alchemy, which is the most fundamental basis for the magical arts because it strengthens the connection between your material body and your higher bodies.

Qigong is a form of moving meditation. Any study of this kind is a useful support for magical work. Now, you may be saying: "Well, our Western witches of the past certainly weren't practicing qigong, were they?" Not as such, perhaps, but in the West, there has been the tradition of prayer and this has not, I suspect, always been seen as a passive act of supplication. It may have involved movements beyond kneeling and folding the hands, as it does in Baptist communities now, for example. Lifting the hands heavenward was a posture of prayer in the ancient Middle East and in Greco-Roman culture. Crossing the hands over the breast was a typical attitude of prayer in Egypt and one that is still used by Freemasons today.

The crane stance is an attitude of magical meditation or prayer employed in the Celtic tradition. It is very reminiscent of qigong. It is a little difficult: balance on one leg and cover the opposite eye with your hand. Another discipline that has many of the same realizations about energy and the body as the Asian arts, is the Western art of fencing with foil or saber. Real fencing is very subtle and complex and is more about feeling what your opponent is going to do rather than brute strength or acrobatics.

In sum, the real use of a wand, like real magic, is not about fighting people in the material world or doing tricks. It is the tool of will, and your best companion whether spiraling over your cauldron or drawing sigils in the air. It will charge magical talismans and serve to enchant whatever it touches, if you have the imagination and integrity of spirit needed to be a real witch.

Wands In Ceremonies

High Priests and priestesses often act as officiants for the ceremonies of life and its passages. The witch's wand plays a part in such ceremonies to indicate who is the director of the ritual. The director may also use a wand to signal others to do their parts—readings and so forth. A wand may be a more integral tool in such ceremonies and may even become a lasting symbol of the passage itself. The four main ceremonies are naming, adulthood rites, handfasting, and passing.

Naming Ceremonies

Naming ceremonies are joyous occasions, welcoming a new person into material existence and giving them a name. The form of the ceremony will, again, vary according to culture or tradition. In many cultures, baptism in some form is used—

dripping water or pouring it over the head of the baby, or briefly immersing a baby or young person. However, touching the child's head with a wand can serve the same purpose for witches and mages. The naming ceremony may come shortly after birth to bestow a legal name, or it may come later as a right of passage into adulthood and a bestowal of a magical name or true name. In either case, water is appropriate as a symbol of purification and beginning. Similarly, a wand can be used to make swirling passes over the child's head in tight, circular motions. This spiraling draws out whatever is considered bad or unfortunate. A tap on the head can carry the new influences for good and plant the seed of virtue.

The name conferred may, of course, be more than just that name by which the child will be called in life. It may be a special magical name carrying the significance of myth or culture. Whatever the case may be, writing this name in sigil form on the forehead of the person being named is an excellent way to seal the action. One may visualize the letters or the sigil of the name in shining blue light. Alternatively, the sign may be made over the heart, or both head and heart.

Adulthood Rites

The Rite of Passage from childhood to adulthood, which is so important in many societies, takes many forms for Pagans in the West today. In most cases, it deals with sexual maturity and so a wand can be employed with its more obvious, literal sexual symbolism. A new name may be added to the child's name, or a completely new adult name be given. The use of the wand to bestow the name is similar to the child's naming. However, the officiant in the ritual may be different. In a child's naming ceremony, the parents may give the name. In adulthood rites it is usually a mentor who is in charge and leads the boy or girl through a type of ordeal. The mysteries of sexuality are revealed in such ceremonies, and at that time, among magical folk, the higher dimensions of sex are also discussed and advice given.

In such rites, whether for boys or girls, the thyrsus and the cup are likely to be used together as masculine and feminine symbols, and as symbols of fire and water, assertion and receptivity. The latter terminology will be more appropriate if the ritual goes beyond explaining heterosexuality and deals with sexuality in all its joyous possibilities.

Handfasting

Although the use of a broom in handfasting is most common, a wand, or especially a staff, could be used as the magical threshold. In her book *The Witch's Broom*, author Deborah Blake suggests that witches might have disguised their magical staff as a broom in order to keep its true nature hidden, which may account for the use of a broom in this tradition.

You will recall I told earlier about the Celtic prince Gwydion who laid a magic wand on the floor for his sister to step over as a test of her truthfulness. In the case of handfasting, the same might be done as a symbolic test of the couple's truth to each other.

A wand can be employed in another way, less fraught with peril. The officiant can tap each of the two betrothed individuals in a manner that is most often associated with the dubbing of a knight. First the left shoulder is touched with the tip of the wand, then the wand is brought to a point just above the head, from which it is lowered again to the right shoulder. As described earlier in the blessing spell, the movement inscribes a triangle around the head of the person who receives this kind of blessing The act draws upon all the power inherent in triangles, denoting all triplicities, whether a triple goddess, or a Divine family of father, mother, and child.

As the gesture is made, you concentrate your mind on the symbolism of the triangle and filling it with the light of blessing and prosperity, charging it with the power current of the law of love, which will bind together those being joined. A simpler gesture of the same kind would be to tap or hold your wand against the cords binding the two hands during the ceremony. A spoken or silent blessing and binding can accompany the gesture. A fully fledged love-binding spell could be used, accompanied by the burning of appropriate incense or anointing the couple with appropriate oils or tinctures. The gesture of tapping with the wand is, as it were, a gesture of completion, a visual "so mote it be."

A longer magic staff may be employed by officiants to lead individuals through the ritual, to lead or direct the members of the audience witnessing the ceremony, and so forth. In such cases, recitation of a spell is not necessary, for the authority and meaning of the rod will be known to those present.

Another use of a wand for couples is to make a special marriage wand that is dedicated to use by both members of the couple together in magical workings. It is a shared wand that brings magic to the union and keeps it active as well as commemorating the handfasting or marriage. There are no special requirements for a marriage wand except that its design should accord with both parties and both parties be aware of its creation. Working together to make the wand would be best of all.

Parting Rites

The rites of parting with friends and loved ones at their death vary from one culture to the next, one religion to the next. Pagans feel the loss of a loved one, but also see the time as one of joy because most believe in some form of afterlife, whether in a new body, in the otherworlds or summerland, or as the individual spirit returns to the Great Spirit of all nature. It is a time not of ending so much as it is a time of transformation. A friend, parent, grandparent, sibling is transformed by passing into one of the ancestors.

The main use of wands here again may be in the rod or staff carried by the attendants. However, a wand can be used by the officiant to make passes over the remains or casket of the deceased. Along with such a gesture, the appropriate prayer or blessing may be included. The officiant can give each member of the family surviving a touch on the head and blessing to relieve their suffering and grief.

A grief wand can be made and dedicated specifically to helping people grieve and heal after a loss. This has wider application than funerals, for we experience many kinds of loss and grief—following the loss of a house, a job, a spouse. Such a wand can be made of yew wood with a reservoir of tourmalinated quartz. It need not be adorned with any ornamentation and may be more twisty than other wands, for it is not so much used to point as to pass over those who mourn.

There is another matter to do with wands and funerals. When a witch or wizard dies, he or she may desire to be buried with his or her wand. Handling this is a delicate matter. The light may or may not have gone from the wand, but the wand and its wielder are so closely bonded that the wand may wish to accompany its mistress or master to the otherworld. If this is the case, it is advised to place the wand in the right hand (that is the dominant hand) of the deceased, angled across the breast, with the left hand resting upon the right.

There is another tradition observed among stage magicians and that is called a Wand Breaking. When the magician dies, his wand is broken at his grave, marking the end to his magic in this world.

Zip *printing & copy shop*

House of Glass

First Term at Four
Hallows

The Alchemist's
Secret

phone (952) 920-2113 • fax (952) 920-8485
www.zipcopyshop.com • e-mail: info@zipcopyshop.com
4950 Excelsior Blvd, St. Louis Park, MN 55416

Wands in
Seasonal Festivals

In this chapter I won't spell out whole rituals for the festivals. Such celebrations should be well-known to the reader. Instead, this section will suggest the places and ways the wand may be used and the components of a wand designed for use in the work of each ceremony. Seasonal rituals link the personal spirit with the anima mundi, the cycles of all nature, which is crucial for higher enlightenment. A modern urban sensibility absorbed with machines and non-natural artifices and environments will have a very hard time engaging with the magical dimensions of nature, just as she might have difficulty trying to raise vegetables. Knowledge of how nature works in the material plane forms the basis for understanding how it works on the other planes—i.e., "magic." The changing seasons and their particular energies are the fundamental structure of these natural forces.

Wanderings: Trees for the Seasons

I USE WANDS whenever I cast a sacred circle and depending on the intent of the ritual I make the choice of what I feel would be the most powerful and effective wood to use. For example, a wand of yew would be ideal for the festival of Samhain and communing with the ancestors. For Autumn Equinox I would possibly use apple for abundance and gratitude and for cleansing and clearing out before the dark half of the year, ivy to break out from restraints or anything holding me back from moving forward with my life, and of course good old silver birch to support any new ventures or relationship beginnings. If I need inspiration or healing, I will sleep with either a willow wand or a hazel wand under my pillow.

—Adrian Rooke, Druid (OBOD)

Note there are eight festivals. We usually think of the year having four seasons, but the Pagan calendar has cross-quarter festivals too, based upon the seasons of agricultural activity. Such activity links human and nature. Even if one is not a farmer or shepherd, partaking in ritual at these four times of the year will attune one with nature and her cycles of birth, growth, harvest, and hibernation.

Samhuinn

Considered the beginning of the New Year by the Celts, Samhuinn (variously spelled) can be translated into English as Summerwane. Samos, the Celtic summer half of the year, comes to its end. On November 1 in the northern latitudes the transformation is sometimes abrupt—from lingering warmth of autumn to the gray cold of winter. Snow may fall, the ground may freeze solid, and then one knows it is time to settle in for the long winter.

Samhuinn is also a harvest festival of sorts. It is the time of the year when the tribe had to cull the herd. Cattle or sheep, had to be evaluated against the amount of fodder produced for them during the grain harvest. How much fodder was there, and how many animals could be fed through the winter with it? All the old animals were slaughtered to reduce the numbers to a size that would survive. This may be part of the reason this sabbat is associated with death, and because of that with our own ancestors. In a sense, each year our own human herd is culled by higher powers as our elders die and pass into the otherworld. At Samhuinn, we can re-establish contact with them as the veils between this world and the other become thin.

A Samhuinn wand has a lot of potential. A ceremonial staff with a skull on top makes perfect sense, and a darker wood is obviously an appropriate choice: black walnut, a lovely chocolate-colored wood; ebony, which may be black or have streaks of brown; or mahogany, a golden brown. Ash is another good choice because of its connection to the Norse World Tree, which is the pathway to all the otherworlds—the worlds of giants and elves, as well as the ancestors. Ash is a white wood but can be stained black for this purpose.

One lovely design for a Samhuinn wand that was made by an apprentice of mine displayed a row of three heads in the handle of the wand, one on top of the other, each head with a primitive face cut into both sides, so that they looked like skulls or specters. Carved from black ebony, it was most effective as a Samhuinn wand and for scrying. In a more light-hearted vein is the pumpkin wand, which incorporates a jack-o'-lantern carved out of wood (or three stacked on top of each other), painted orange and black. A larger pumpkin-head can be carved and placed on the end of a ceremonial wand carved with pumpkin leaves and vines. The bottom of the wand—its pommel—is a large egg shaped of black stone. The weight of this stone (a simple water-smoothed rock from a lake shore or river or a polished egg) gives the rod a balance like the pendulum of a clock, which alludes to time.

Black and orange have become the colors of Hallowe'en, the Eve of Samhuinn, also known as All Hallows Eve, a Pagan-Christian crossover. Black and white are also suitable being the color of darkness and the color of bare bones. Incorporating bone into a Samhuinn wand is another possibility. A bone could serve as the body of the wand; however, I prefer to take a wood such as ash, which is fairly white, and carve it to look like a bone. There are varying opinions on the use of animal parts in rituals. On the other hand, Samhuinn provides the one time when using the bone of a sacrificed animal is actually appropriate. Make it an animal killed for its meat in order to connect with your ancestors and the life cycle of earlier times before freezers and refrigerators.

All this said, it is yew wood that is the most often used in Samhuinn wands. Traditionally planted in churchyards, yew trees are another evergreen. They are also the tree of the seers and have particular power to contact ancestral spirits. A yew wand may be used ceremonially to open the veils. Juniper is another evergreen with similar properties, the energy of eternal life.

Midwinter (Yule)

If Midsummer was the triumphal time of the Oak King, Midwinter or Yule is the time we celebrate the equally important peak of the Holly King's rule. As I noted earlier, you can take this different ways. Is the turn of the solstice the triumph of the Holly King because it is his high point? Or the triumph of the new Oak King, whose coming is heralded by the turning of the sun from north to south at the solstice? Holly is the tree most associated with Yule (along with mistletoe, which is really more of a shrub or herb). I take it to be the festival of the Holly King. His leaves are evergreen and so symbolize the triumph and persistence of life through the dark winter. His berries are first white and then red, symbolizing death and rebirth. I also consider the holly tree to live in a kind of symbolic balance with the rowan. The latter brings forth berries that start greenish white and turn darker orange as summer passes, giving food to the birds sometimes even when winter descends (if they haven't already eaten them as they migrated south). Rowan is not evergreen, however, and so cannot serve as a winter tree of life.

The wood of the holly tree makes beautiful wands and carries the energy of loyalty, steadfastness, self-assertion, protection, and continuation—because of its evergreen leaves. Other evergreens are also used at this time of year: pine, fir, cedar—all have their place as trees of symbolic life-in-death, abiding green through the winter months. So, the Yule tree or Christmas tree serves to bring the power of the evergreen conifers into the home to empower that persistence of the light through the darkness and life through death.

A Yule wand or staff should capture these features, not only by being made out of such trees, but by being decorated with them as well. A holly wand twined with mistletoe is about as Yulish as you can get, though probably you will put on fresh mistletoe each year. Again, the antlers of the Stag of Summer can be appropriate because a solar god lies at the center of this rebirth story.

Branches of pine or fir must be carefully dried before being carved into a wand because of their sticky sap. Crowned or tipped with a pinecone, this wand, like the thyrsus at Beltane, serves to remind us of the hidden fertility at the time of winter solstice. The two wands can be distinguished by painting the pinecone of the Beltane wand red; and painting the pinecone of the Yule wand gold. The sun, source of life, lies symbolically within the womb of the Mother Earth in winter, and emerges (or stirs toward his birth) at this time. Gold decorations on the wand draw upon the symbolism of the sun-seed.

Imbolc

Known as the feast of Candlemas and of the goddess/saint Brigit or Bride (pronounced *Breed*), Imbolc is the middle of winter in some parts of the northern hemisphere. In the British, Irish, Manx, and Scottish Isles, the weather being relatively clement, February 1 was a time to note the "first stirrings" of life. We retain this idea in the American Groundhog Day. Originally hedgehogs, the day marked a sort of general time when it was expected little hibernating animals would come out of their holes to check on the progress of spring.

For a Pagan celebration of Imbolc a wand dedicated to the goddess Bride would be most appropriate. I would make such a wand from rowan or birch wood with a reservoir stone of angelite or tree agate. The former stone is periwinkle blue, the latter white with green veins. Angelite links Bride to her role as the patroness of poetry and bards, whose robes are blue in many Druid traditions. Tree agate alludes to two other aspects of Bride: her association with purity (the white stone) and her reputation as a healer (the green veins, green being one of the colors of life representing herbs and the vegetal world). Rowan is a tree that often preserves its orange berries through the winter, feeding birds, and symbolizing the continuity of life though death—that is rebirth—so central to this time of year. Birch is also associated with beginnings and with bards, so is a particularly sacred wood for Bride and Imbolc. Finish them as lightly as possible to preserve a whiteness.

Alternatively, they could be painted white. Birch leaves could be carved upon the handle or shaft for a further association; or likewise, a Brigit's cross, a traditional Celtic emblem of Imbolc.

Such an Imbolc wand can be used to spiral energy over newly sprouted herbs or grass, newborn lambs (or any kind of newborn), or over a small fire, like a candle. Spiraling upward and outward—that is, enlarging the spiral upward—signifies the growth and extension of the emerging spring.

Bride wand with tree agate

Wands in Seasonal Festivals

Vernal Equinox (Ostara)

A wand for Ostara can be made of apple wood or almond—lighter fruitwoods with spring blossoms. Most appropriately it may be tipped with an egg. In such a case, the egg symbolizes birth, which is only just beginning at this time of year. The egg symbolizes the power of reproductive energy, but not only re-production, it also represents production, the creation of something new. Thus the "Easter egg" as a symbol of rebirth or "rising from the dead." Spring is the time of year when we most strongly think about the cycle of life and its fundamental quality—that of being able to produce others of its kind.

This power of the cosmic egg is the female energy of creation, so a wand wood for Ostara should have that feminine vibration, and in this case water rather than earth. Water is the feminine element, infinitely malleable, filling in wherever the low spots are in the earth (the other feminine, receptive element). Water is also the vast mystery of the sea, the original source of living things, and the power of the oceans that sets all weather at work, and so creates climate. Water is a destructive force as well as a life-giving force. Our bodies are 90% water, yet submerged for just a few minutes, we perish.

So, tree types to use for Ostara wands are willow and birch. Both are most strongly attuned to elemental water. Willow is the supreme "witch wood" and birch is dedicated to new beginnings. A birch wand is appropriate to use when beginning any operation or phase of life. Willow is valued for its property of "weaving." This means the weaving together of energies into a pattern that can be cast as a spell. Birch is dedicated to Bride, the White Goddess, and willow expressly to the moon—Diana, Luna, Selene, Artemis.

Ostara egg wand

Beltane

Cherry wood might be a nice choice for Beltane, a passionate and fecund time. Cherry with its pink blossoms radiates love, but the heartwood of the branches is a silky red that grows more red the longer it is exposed to sunlight. Thus it is sacred to Ares, not as god of war but as guardian and lover of Aphrodite. Ares is a god similar to the fiery Bel of the Celts, as well as the Phoenicians of the Middle East. Bel, after whom the festival is obviously named, is the Eye of the Sun. I think of him more as the god of primordial fire, like Hindu Agni—a god behind passion and heat, the natural force rather than the image of armored Ares or Mars. Beltane signifies the beginning of the summer season.

The tree most associated with Beltane is the hawthorn, or whitethorn. It is a thorn and so sacred to the folk of Faery, but not quite as dangerous as blackthorn. Its white five-petaled blossoms are called May flowers and are associated with sexual relations because of the erotic quality of their scent. Hawthorn is a wonderful wand wood and a branch on the stocky side, with a phallic shape that suits Beltane. An appropriate stone, carnelian has fiery qualities; or rose quartz for its evocation of Eros—depending on what nuance of the season's frolics one wishes to bring out. A serpent could be carved climbing up the wand's shaft. A point made of deer antler would also be a good touch for a Beltane wand as it is often associated with Cernunnos, the antlered god of the Celts.

Additionally, a thyrsus wand would be a fine Beltane wand for its revels and dancing—a shaft of pine or spruce with a large pinecone for its tip. It is held by the opposite end with the pinecone upward. Attaching a pinecone would have to be done mostly with glue. You could try fixing a pin into the top of the wand and the bottom of the pinecone, then gluing them.

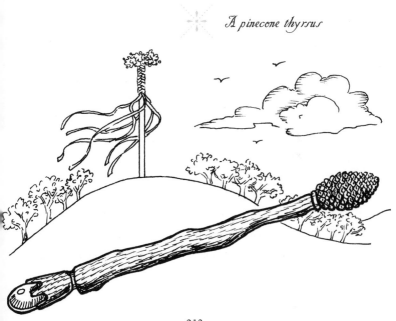

A pinecone thyrsus

Wands in Seasonal Festivals

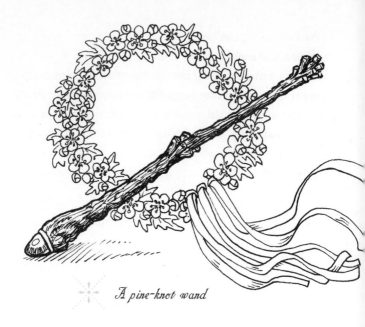

Another sort of wand you might like to try for this phallic shape is made by keeping your Yule tree and, before Beltane, cutting off its branches close to the trunk. In many evergreens the branches cluster together and emerge at distinct levels. When the trunk is cut up into pieces the top couple of sections are about the right size for a thyrsus-type wand. The slender part of the section is the handle, and when all the branch ends are cut down to the knot, it forms a sort of club head.

A Beltane wand is best used to make the circle for the celebration and consecrate the fire. The gesture for fire consecration is a more swirling motion from the center of the fire outward. The wand may be traded between members of the opposite sex within the group as a symbolic gift of fertility. It may be held by an officiant of the ceremony to lead the procession or to signal individuals or couples who are jumping the Beltane fire.

Summer Solstice (Midsummer)

Midsummer is the festival of the Oak King and so a wand of oak is the most appropriate. Oak wands usually have a twisty rather than perfectly straight form and have both beautiful thick bark and distinct coarse (and hard) grain. So, you can take the bark off or leave it on, according to taste. Clear quartz crystal is a fine complement to oak for general purposes. A wand dedicated especially to the summer solstice might like a reservoir stone of honey calcite (which looks just like amber) or red agate. Orange-yellow is more evocative of the sun than red, which is the color of Mars, so stones with this tint would be appropriate. Gold is the metal sacred to the sun, but a large reservoir of solid gold would probably be too expensive for most. Gold inlay would be fabulous if you can afford it. As far as a reservoir stone like gold, pyrite can be a possibility. If you can find pyrite (also called "fool's gold") in the right shape and size for your oak wand, that could be a lovely combination.

As far as carving and symbolism goes, the point within the circle that is the symbol of the sun is most important. Any circle with rays extending from it might serve too. However, in any carving, you will be fighting the coarse grain of oak. Not only is it hard to carve; its darkness obscures carved designs. So, a simple inscription to the god or goddess of the sun might be the best thing. (It will be obscured, but a kind of subtly hidden inscription like that is nice in a case like this.)

In ritual, at Midsummer, often oak-leaf crowns are one of the props. An oak wand can be used to bless the participants. For this kind of blessing, taking a long wand and touching each shoulder of the person reflects the Sun King's kingliness.

Some groups enact the battle between the Oak King and the Holly King at Midsummer (though it is more often done at Midwinter). At this time of year, the battle symbolizes the Oak King at the height of his powers, yet defeated by the Holly King, who then becomes the king for the winter half of the year. While it is traditional for this battle to happen at the solstices, there is a logic for performing them instead at the beginning of summer and the beginning of winter (which is to say at Beltane and Samhuinn).

I think that at the solstices, the symbolic battle between the forces of summer and winter reminds us in each case

Wands in Seasonal Festivals

that the one contains the beginnings of the other. Especially at Yule do we wish to be reassured that deadly winter will end, but the Holly King's triumph over the Oak King at midsummer dramatizes the division of the year into two seasons: one light and one dark. These are called Samos (summer) and Giamos (not summer)—Samhuinn can thus be translated as Summerwane, the end of Samos. You may have guessed that the Oak and Holly Kings are two aspects of one entity, and a wand for this season may rightly bear carvings of oak and holly leaves.

Lammas (Lunasa)

At the festival of Lammas or Lunasa (or Lughnasadh, as it is in Irish Gaelic), the sun's fruitfulness is still evident. It is the celebration of the first harvest of grain and the making of bread. What kind of a wand would one make for Lammas? You can go in many directions. Apple is appropriate for this time of year since the apple harvest is beginning soon and is also one of the fruits of the earth. Apple is a tree of the Fair Folk too.

I am drawn to elm as the Mother-Tree in this festival and I will tell you why. There is a Celtic association between this festival and a story of a pregnant mother. It is a rather sad story (as most Celtic songs are), but it involves her fulfilling a dare. Tailtu was the foster mother of the god Lugh (aka

Lugos). She was a fantastic runner and someone or other bet that she could outrun the king's horses. Bad timing, as she was pregnant. She won but died as a result. In her honor and memory, Lugh established the Tailteann Games, held at Lunasa, which consisted especially of horse races. Now, Tailtu was a tough cookie and elm is a goddess tree that has particularly hard wood. The elm's shape is that of a chalice, with branches gracefully curved upwards.

Stones to consider for a Lunasa wand are tree agate or moss agate, jade, serpentine, or aventurine, all green in color. These all are appropriate for the Festival of the Harvest.

So, an apple or elm wand carved with horse designs of a Celtic interlace type would be delightful as a Lunasa wand. It could be carved with apples and with heads of wheat and barley. Ceremonially, a wand might be used in a number of ways depending on what was going on. If you put on games and races, the Lunasa wand is perfect for starting those races and even for "dubbing" the winner on each shoulder.

There is another approach to Lunasa that is brought in by our culture's associating this time with the beginning of school (usually a bit later at September but within this season). The harvest season is the ending of summer at a family farm. The fall harvest is one of the main reasons school-starting time is after Lunasa. Associating school with the season of Lugh makes sense. Lugh is the Samildanach, meaning the one who masters all arts. He knows everything and can practice any art or craft. His magical weapon (one of the Four Treasures of the Tuatha Dé Danann) is a spear that can be sent out, and will automatically (as it were) kill the enemy until recalled.

The spear is one of the interpretations of the tarot suit of wands. In some decks we find spears or quarterstaffs depicted. So, Lugh's spear is a symbol of the wand and its power of assertive will. Expressed in the primal form of "killing enemies" we can think of this as the more general act of overcoming obstacles and challenges, or penetrating falsehoods to find truth.

Autumnal Equinox (Mabon)

Autumn in North America is particularly signaled by the sugar maple trees changing their leaves to bright colors. This display of beauty prior to the falling of the leaves for winter is a wonder of our world. It is not something everyone in the world can experience, but in the northern forests of the world summer gives way to winter gradually and the transition time of autumn is full of meaning. It responds first by a burst of beauty before falling into its winter sleep. For this reason, trees that change color vividly in the autumn are the ones best suited for a wand dedicated to Mabon. Maple is my favorite choice.

The equinox also symbolizes balance between the opposites of light and dark. Day and night are conceived in this view as two halves of a whole, as are summer and winter. The waning of the light half of year and the waxing of darkness (if we can put it that way) is celebrated at Mabon. This is not so much a celebration of harvest as a solar festival that marks the turning of the solar year. Mabon, in the old Celtic myths, was a kind of solar hero: Mabon, son of Modron, which literally means child, son of the mother. Neither light nor darkness are triumphant at this moment. They are in balance. Darkness and the cold are descending upon the world, but life responds with an explosion of color and beauty. A wand designed for Mabon should reflect this balance, so one half may be stained dark, the other light. I prefer the dark half to be red, the light half yellow-gold.

Likewise, a point of clear quartz can be balanced by a pommel stone of jet-black obsidian or red jasper. You could build it the other way too: with the shaft light and the handle dark, the pommel stone light and the crystal point dark. In that case, I should choose milky quartz for the pommel and a cut point of a black stone.

Mabon is also associated with Cernunnos the stag-god, so antler points are appropriate, if you like. You may cut a curve of antler so that you have a crescent. The blunt end could be shaped to a point, but I like to leave it as is. Then, carve the point end of the wood wand into a fork that will go around the antler. It and the shaft are wrapped in an infinity pattern with sinew. In this case, you have a ceremonial wand that

A crescent antler wand

bears the symbol of the moon with the symbol of the stag, male and female divinity united in one. The white antler can be balanced by a dark pommel stone, say bloodstone or jasper.

So, we have walked the wheel of the year and return to the beginning as Samhuinn. If you have wands specially made for each of these festivals, you and your coven will be well prepared to take them out and add them to your rituals as a special sign of the season. The witch's wand, as you have seen, can be an ever-present tool for Witchcraft, useful in so many ways.

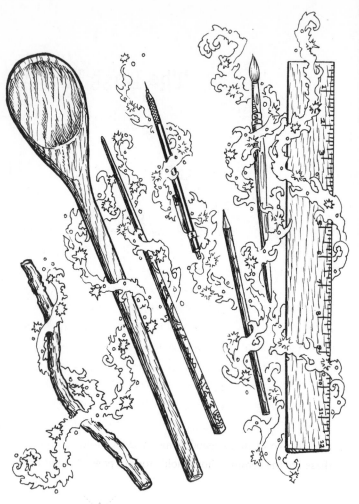

*The magical life is filled
with wands of all sorts!*

The Last Word

I end these thoughts on the witch's wand by considering, after all the ceremonial possibilities, the homely wand. Alone at home, a witch carries her wand for constant blessing and cleansing work. Never dismiss the utility of a spell to keep the house clean or protect it from harm. Spells used in cooking are common, too, and casting them with a wand dedicated to the culinary arts acknowledges the magic of food and fire.

You cannot fix a drain or a broken blender with your wand, but you can cast preventative maintenance spells to avert such inconveniences. (I have yet to develop a reliable spell that will keep windows from getting dirty...)

A feather duster, a wooden spoon, even a toilet plunger—these are the common household "rods of power" along with the broomstick. Consider how they may be augmented magically. In the end, a wand is more than a tool for ritual. It is a constant companion, a familiar spirit, and a source of stability and tree-wisdom in the magical life.

Appendices

Table I:
Trees and Their Magical Qualities

TREE	ELEMENT/KEY	SACRED TO	MAGICAL PROPERTIES
Alder	Water Preserving	Pisces, Deirdre, Bran	Oracular magic, seership, dreamwork, preservation, concealment, bridging worlds
Apple	Air Singing	Lunasa, Rhiannon, Epona, Pwyll, King Arthur, Avalon, Venus, Throat Chakra	Protection, blessing, calling, sending, opening doorways to other worlds, love, inspiration, enchantment
Ash	Earth and Water Journeying	Virgo, Artemis, Diana, Mercury, Llyr	Calling, direction of art and craft, moving toward a goal, healing, crossing bridges to other worlds

Tree	Element/Key	Sacred To	Magical Properties
Beech	Fire Learning	Mercury, Minerva, Lugh, Ogma, Belinos, Sun, Solar Plexus Chakra	Solar and positive magic, the enhancement of creativity, learning, the search for information, books, languages
Birch	Water Beginning	Vernal Equinox, Spring, Flora, Bards	Purification, discipline, spells of youth and fresh starts, creativity, procreation, birth, renewal and rebirth
Blackthorn and Plum	Earth Blocking	Babh, the Crone, Pluto, Hades	Protection, Faerie magic, overcoming creative barriers, persistence, patience, divining of precious metals
Cedar	Air Cleansing	Imbolc, Brigid	Enchantment, clearing negativity, dedication of sacred space, poetry, smithcraft, healing
Cherry	Fire Desiring	Mars/Ares, Aries, Teutates	Protection, conflict, sex, attraction, assertiveness, aggression, love, confidence, daring, union of opposites, root chakra, healing of injuries from conflict or loss

TREE	ELEMENT/KEY	SACRED TO	MAGICAL PROPERTIES
Chestnut	Water Producing	Zeus, Gaia, Ouranos, Aphrodite, Cancer, Dana, Naiads, Undines	Fertility, feminine powers, motherhood, the sea, protection of waters, reflection, introspection, meditation, abundance, nurturance, cleansing, relationships, especially mother and child
Ebony	Earth Dominating	Hekate, Dark Moon, Pluto/ Hades, Circe, Cerridwen, Arawn	Leadership, domination, penetrating to the core of any problem, control, sexual assertion, aggression, concealing, revealing, healing dark diseases, dragon energy, seduction
Elder	Earth Regenerating	Taurus, Venus, Boann	Enchantment, healing, protection, regeneration, wealth, long life, nurturing
Elm	Earth Containing	Saturn, Dana	Healing, fertility, growth rebirth, destiny, wisdom, metamorphosis, endurance
Hawthorn	Air Guarding	Aquarius, the White Hart, the Green Man, Bealtaine	Fertility, rebirth, renewal union, wildness, human being as animal, detects magic, counter-jinxes, warding, sending

TREE	ELEMENT/KEY	SACRED TO	MAGICAL PROPERTIES
Hazel	Air Understanding	The White Goddess, Arianrhod, the Full Moon, Sophia, the Salmon of Wisdom, Virgo	Female autonomy, feminine power, magic of wisdom, beauty, charm, love, navigation, summoning, attraction, creativity
Holly	Fire Penetrating	Holly King, Hades, Arawn, Persephone, Demeter	Protection, work against evil spirits, poisons, angry elementals, and lightning; averting fear, allowing courage to emerge, dream magic and eternal life, success in business or endeavor, hunting or quests
Juniper	Earth Transforming	The Morrigan, the Cailleach, Samhuinn	Transformation, transition, crossing to other worlds, cloaking, revealing, letting go, yin power, shadow, meditation, seduction, binding, geas, fate
Lilac	Air Imagining	Mercury, Gemini, Gwydion, Vernal Equinox	Magic of union, attraction, cultivation of creative bliss, intellectual pursuits, imagination, information, mental power, creation of harmony, travel, illusion, detection, writing

Tree	Element/Key	Sacred To	Magical Properties
Linden	Air Attracting	Deirdre, Oengus Og, Eros, Aphrodite, Heart Chakra	Creation, transmutation, illumination, love, attraction, binding, obligation, healing wounds, enhancement of beauty, peace
Maple	Earth and Fire Changing	Autumnal Equinox, Libra and Virgo, John Barleycorn, Green Man, Mabon son of Modron, Cerridwen, the Moon, Minerva	Control, finding, binding, transformation, creation, ambition, passion, revolution, rebirth, poetry, beauty, harvest, healing, abundance
Oak	Fire Opening	Leo, Sun, Center, Ogma, Hu, Arthur, Belinos, Apollo	Leadership, wise rule, personal sovereignty, authority, power, protection, sealing or opening doors, endurance, invocation of wisdom, fertility, abundance
Poplar	Water Feeling	Arianrhod, Dylan, Poseidon, Proteus, Psyche	Emotions, feelings, sensitivity, intuition, empathy, dance, instincts

TREE	ELEMENT/KEY	SACRED TO	MAGICAL PROPERTIES
Redwood	Fire Aspiring	Cernunnos, Stag of Summer, Gaia, Sagittarius, Chiron	Striving upward, travel to higher spheres, drawing down power from heaven to earth, religious seeking, discipline, mystical union, wild animals, wisdom
Rowan	Earth Quickening	Capricorn, Winter Solstice, Govannon the Smith, Brighid, Pan, Belly Chakra	Unites fire and earth elements, bridges worlds, astral vision, protection, warding off evil spirits, averts storms and lightning (sudden disaster and struggle), brings peace, growth, fertility, rebirth; supports women's autonomy, poetry, metalwork, geomancy, work with ley lines
Spruce, also Fir and Pine	Water Turning	Winter Solstice, Arawn, Pwyll, Hades, Cerridwen, Hecate	Battling evil, astral flight, cleansing, purification, creation, potion-making, witches brooms, transformation, shape shifting, wisdom

TREE	ELEMENT/KEY	SACRED TO	MAGICAL PROPERTIES
Walnut	Air and Fire Illuminating	Jupiter, Mercury, Taranis, Odin, Minerva, Crown Chakra	Wind and weather magic, expansion, vortices, enhancement of the powers of breath, spells to conjure or avert lightning, hurricanes or cyclones; teleportation, astral travel, knowledge, wisdom
Willow	Water Weaving	The Moon, Luna, Phoebe, Diana, Artemis, Selene, Hecate, Cerridwen, Arachne	Dowsing, divination, seership, rain-making, funerary rites, love, easing childbirth, fertility, healing, glamour, bewitchment, concealment, secrecy, germination, herb-magic, potion-making, melody and combination
Yew	Air and Earth Remembering	Arawn, Maeve, Hermes, Hecate, the Dagda	Death, grieving, travel between worlds, ancestors, trance, seership, divination, healing, transformation, knowledge, eloquence, persuasion, mediumism, necromancy

Table II:
Magical Powers of Stones and Metals

Mineral & Color	Planet, Deity, Sign	Magical Properties
Agate, Banded Red and Brown	Mercury, Gemini	Protection, victory, attracting love, promoting fertility, turning away lightning or evil spirits, finding buried treasure, curing insomnia, giving pleasant dreams
Agate, Tree White	Mercury	Purification, light, branching paths of causation and choice
Agate, Moss Green	Taurus, Venus, Gemini	Eloquence, persuasion, fertility, magnetism, eternal life, knowledge, astral travel, scrying, contacting spirit guide
Amber Golden	Sun	Excellent fluid condenser, combining yin and yang, protection, attraction, sensuality
Amethyst Purple	Aquarius	Averts intoxication, protection against losing oneself, losing control, or false infatuations; clairvoyance, prescience, dispelling illusions

MINERAL & COLOR	PLANET, DEITY, SIGN	MAGICAL PROPERTIES
Aventurine Green	Earth	Protection, good luck in gambling, releases anxieties, inspires independence and positive attitudes; enhances visualization, writing, art, music
Bloodstone Green and Red	Mars	Links root and heart chakras, preserves health, creates abundance, self-confidence; lengthens life, gives fame, aids invisibility, removes obstacles
Calcite Multicolored	Venus	Clears negative energies, intensifies mental and emotional clarity, attracts love
Carnelian Red	Mars/Ares, Aries	Protects against the evil eye, fulfills all desires, speeds manifestations, revitalizes the body and spirit, strengthens concentration
Citrine Yellow-gold or Clear	Mercury, Pluto, Scorpio	Protects against intoxication, evil thoughts, overindulgence, snakes, plagues, epidemics; gives clarity of thought, aligns ego with higher self

Mineral & Color	Planet, Deity, Sign	Magical Properties
Fluorite Multicolored	Pisces and Capricorn	Grounds excessive energy, enhances astral senses, healing through chakras, enhances abstract understanding, meditation, studying, dreaming
Hematite Shiny Gray	Mars, Aries, Aquarius	Aids in favorable hearings or judgments, in winning petitions before those in authority; protects warriors, energizes the etheric body, gives optimism, confidence, and courage
Jade Green	Aries, Gemini, Libra	Strengthens the heart, kidneys, and immune system; increases fertility, cleanses etherically, balances the emotions, dispels negativity, gives courage and wisdom
Jasper Red or Brown	Jupiter	Weatherworking, bringing rain, curing wounds, healing stomach ailments; balances chakras, stabilizes energy, protects from negativity; dispels hallucinations, evil spirits, and nightmares

MINERAL & COLOR	PLANET, DEITY, SIGN	MAGICAL PROPERTIES
Labradorite Gray Rainbow Chatoyant	Neptune, Poseidon, Proteus, Thetis	Sea and ocean magic, deep unconscious, mists and mysteries, solving and dispelling, dissolving, immersion of feelings
Lapis Lazuli Dark Blue and White with Gold Specks	Jupiter, Isis	Opens the throat chakra, removes painful memories, brings good fortune, releases tension and anxiety, increases mental clarity, creativity, and clairvoyance; helps overcome depression and aids communication with spirit guides
Malachite Green Stripes	Venus, Minerva	Gives ability to understand animal languages, protects, revitalizes body and mind, repels evil spirits, inspires tolerance and flexibility, opens communication, stabilizes energy
Moonstone White to Pink Chatoyant	Moon, Artemis, Diana, Cancer	Moon magic, mothers, family, astral travel, hunting/seeking, healing, change, dreams, unconscious feelings

Mineral & Color	Planet, Deity, Sign	Magical Properties
Onyx Black, White, or Brown Banded	Saturn, Gaia	Balances male and female polarities, gives spiritual inspiration, helps face past life problems and transformational challenges; expands the imagination, deflects negative energy
Quartz Crystal Clear and Colorless	The Zenith and the Center	Amplifies etheric energies, draws together the divine sphere and the material sphere; enhances meditation and communication with spirits, telepathy, clairvoyance, and visualization
Rose Quartz Translucent Pink	Venus, Libra	Creates love, heals the emotions, gives compassion, reduces anxiety, enhances creativity and self-confidence; resonant to the heart chakra
Smoky Quartz Grayish brown, Translucent	Pluto	Attuned to the root chakra, aids in meditation by grounding and centering; helps transform dreams into material manifestation; breaks through blockages

Mineral & Color	Planet, Deity, Sign	Magical Properties
Milky Quartz Translucent White	Moon, Cancer	Nurtures feminine energies, promotes good spirit guides for astral travel; also freedom for women and their independence; all workings to do with mothers or emotions
Quartz, Rutilated Translucent Gray, with Threadlike Inclusions	Venus, Thetis, Gemini, Taurus	Enhances life energy, increases clairvoyance, transmutes negative energy, aids in communication with one's higher self, increases the efficacy of magic
Quartz, Tourmalinated Clear with Inclusions of Tourmaline	Moon, Cancer	Absorbs negativity, grounds, balances, protects, dispels grief and sorrow, heals traumas, transforms emotions
Rhodonite Pink with Veins or Patches of Gray or Black	Isis, Minerva	Reduces stress, calms the mind, enhances energy and vitality, deters interruptions; maximum potential, emotional healing, love; wisdom, quests

MINERAL & COLOR	PLANET, DEITY, SIGN	MAGICAL PROPERTIES
Serpentine Opaque Mottled Green	Mercury, Persephone	Protection against deception, attack, offense; increases prudence and self-restraint; indirect travel, quests, increasing knowledge and wisdom; re-emerging
Tiger's-Eye Chatoyant Striped Yellow, Gold, Brown	Hercules, Leo	Protection, courage; strengthens emotions, eliminate fears and anxieties; grounding, centering; strengthens the will, self-confidence, luck; stored assertiveness
Turquoise Sky Blue or Light Green	Venus, Jupiter, Egyptian Hathor and Celtic Boann	Conducting energy from one person or place to another, attraction, abundance, elemental air; brings love and prosperity, green magic or blue magic

Table III:
Beast Symbolism

Many are the mythical beasts that wander the moors and mountains of the astral plane. They are the beasts of dream who speak to us, who guide us from one world to another, and who counsel us or thwart us, according to our merits and intentions. Here is a summary of the creatures whose hair, skin, or feather is most often used in wands.

CREATURE/PART	CHARACTER AND QUALITIES
Dragon Scale	Use a splinter or shard of a scale. Light will vary depending on the color of the dragon. Black has strong ultraviolet. Red for passion, protection, vengeance. Green for prosperity, earthworking, treasure-finding, and finding spells generally. Black to intensify intelligence, cunning, and vision into other worlds. Gold for weatherworking, prosperity, wisdom, guidance, friendship, and fertility.
Gryphon Feather or Hair	Sacred to Nemesis, the Hellenic goddess of vengeance. Symbolizes high nobility and power. Has the hearing of dogs and the eyesight of eagles; feline temperament, carnivorous, sudden and aggressive, deadly; king of beasts and monarch of the skies combined; royal, loyal guards of treasures, spiritual riches. Has the power of vigilance, ferocity, perception, strength, dependability, clairvoyance, wisdom, clairaudience and, on the negative side, avarice. (See Nigg in the bibliography for more.)

CREATURE/PART	CHARACTER AND QUALITIES
Hippogriff Feather or Hair	The wild energy of running or flying free—taking a determined path or soaring into the realms of imagination. Union of opposites. Aggressiveness, assertiveness, eagerness to help. Actions of elemental air or earth—the mental and material. Mind-body healing.
Hippocampus Hair	Watery magic, works to combine elemental water and earth. Emotional and physical healing, developing clairvoyance, prophecy, imaginal vision and dreams. Strength, service, calm.
Phoenix Feather	Spirit of fire, renewal, death and rebirth, endurance, healing. Also, hope for immortality and the power of beauty to enchant. Transformative passion, remaking oneself. Herbivores, gentle and intelligent. Very strong healing powers, enhancing the power of the will, and treating fevers, physical or emotional.
Spirit Owl Feather	Minerva-Athena. Wisdom, assertion, aggression, protection, disguise, secret aid. Also, digestion, cleansing, secrecy, and stealth.
Spirit Raven Feather	Odin and the war goddess Babh. Wisdom, cunning, intelligence, spying, making good of something seemingly dead. Vision flight. Conflict resolution. Swiftness in thought, action, and self-protection. Prospering at someone else's expense; business dealings, and opportunities.
Spirit Snake Skin	Wisdom and healing, especially white snakes. Represented in a spiral or helix, snakes can symbolize the whole cosmos.

CREATURE/PART	CHARACTER AND QUALITIES
Unicorn Hair	Aggressive, protective, pure, integrity of spirit, and unspoiled essence. Able to cleanse all poisons with its horn. Nobility of spirit, the untamable spirit of the horse; service to women and true virtue. Healing disease and detecting poisons. Finding treasures, purifying. Creates all virtues: love, faith, hope, justice, wisdom, truth, and fortitude. Attuned to the Divine Feminine. (See Beer in the bibliography for more.)
Spirit Wolf Fur	The wolf is a magical animal even in this dimension, but the spirit wolf embodies the powers of the moon, wildness and wilderness, freedom, protection, aggression, loyalty, affection to one's own, and cooperation with others. May be a powerful male or female energy.

Bibliography

AE (George William Russell). "The Many-Colored Land" in *The Candle of Vision* (1918), www.sacred-texts.com.

Agrippa, Henry Cornelius. *Three Books of Occult Philosophy.* Llewellyn's Sourcebook Series. Edited by Donald Tyson. Llewellyn, 1992.

Buckland, Raymond. *Buckland's Complete Book of Witchcraft.* Llewellyn, 1992.

Bardon, Franz. *Initiation into Hermetics: A Course of Instruction of Magic Theory and Practice.* Translated by A. Radspieler. Dieter Rüggeberg, 1981.

Barrabbas, Frater. *Mastering the Art of Ritual Magic: Foundation, Grimoire, and The Greater Key.* Megalithica Books, 2013.

Beer, Rüdiger Robert. *Unicorn: Myth and Reality.* Translated by Charles M. Stern. Van Nostrand Reinhold, 1972.

Black, Susa Morgan. "Blackthorn," http://www
.druidry.org/obod/trees/blackthorn.html.

Blamires, Steve. *Celtic Tree Mysteries: Secrets of the Ogham.*
Llewellyn, 1998.

Blaxell, Claudia. *Spellbinding: Spells and Rituals that Will
Empower Your Life.* Hay House, 2001.

Bonewits, Philip Emmons Isaac. *Real Magic: An Introductory
Treatise on the Basic Principles of Yellow Magic.* Revised
Edition. Creative Arts Book Co., 1971.

Budapest, Zsuzsanna. *The Holy Book of Women's Mysteries.*
Weiser Books, 2007.

Bulfinch, Thomas. *Bulfinch's Mythology: The Age of Fable*
(1855), www.sacred-texts.com.

Carr-Gomm, Philip. *Druidcraft: The Magic of Wicca and
Druidry.* Thorsons, 2002; CreateSpace, 2013.

Conway, D. J. *Crystal Enchantments: A Complete Guide to
Stones and Their Magical Properties.* Crossing Press, 1999.

Cooper, Phillip. *Basic Sigil Magic.* Weiser Books, 2001.

Couzens, Reginald C. *The Stories of Months and Days* (1923),
www.sacred-texts.com/time/smd/smd07.htm.

Cunningham, Scott. *Cunningham's Encyclopedia of Crystal,
Gem & Metal Magic.* Llewellyn, 1988.

———. *Earth Magic.* Llewellyn, 2000.

———. *Wicca; Living Wicca; The Complete Book of Incense, Oils, and Brews.* One-volume edition. One Spirit, 1988.

Dolnick, Barrie. *Simple Spells for Success: Ancient Practices for Creating Abundance and Prosperity.* Harmony Books, 1996.

DuQuette, Lon Milo. *Homemade Magick: The Musings and Mischief of a Do-It-Yourself Magus.* Llewellyn, 2014.

Evans-Wentz, W. Y. *The Fairy-Faith in Celtic Countries* (1911), www.sacred-texts.com/neu/celt/ffcc/ffcc260.htm.

Flaccus, Valerius. *Argonautica.* Trans. Mozley. (Roman epic, circa AD 1, ch. 7, p. 210 ff. referring to Aphrodite in disguise as Circe.)

Friedlander, Walter J. *The Golden Wand of Medicine: A History of the Caduceus Symbol in Medicine.* New York: Greenwood Press, 1992.

Gardner, Gerald. *The Garderian Book of Shadows.* Edited by Aidan Kelly. Internet Book of Shadows. Original date: 1949. Edited edition dated: approx. 1990, www.sacred-texts.com/pag/gbos/index.htm.

Goblet d'Alviella. *The Migration of Symbols* (1894). University Books, 1956 (reprint).

Grimassi, Raven. *Hereditary Witchcraft: Secrets of the Old Religion.* Llewellyn, 1999.

Guest, Lady Charlotte, Trans. *The Mabinogion* (1877), www.sacred-texts.com.

Hall, Manly. *Secret Teachings of All Ages* (1928). Tarcher, reprint edition, 2003.

Homer. *Odyssey*.

Illes, Judica. *The Element Encyclopedia of 5000 Spells*. Element Books, 2004.

Imuhtuk on The Lotus Wand, www.angelfire.com/ab6/imuhtuk/gdmans/wand/wang.htm.

Jacobs, Joseph. *English Fairy Tales* (1890), www.sacred-texts.com/neu/eng/eft/eft24.htm.

Jacoilliot, Louis. *Occult Science in India* (1919), www.sacred-texts.com/eso/osi/osi12.htm.

K, Amber. *True Magic: A Beginner's Guide.* Llewellyn, 1990.

Kendall, Paul. "Mythology and Folklore of the Alder," http://www.treesforlife.org.uk/forest/mythfolk/alder.html.

———. "Mythology and Folklore of the Willow," http://www.treesforlife.org.uk/forest/mythfolk/willow.html.

The Key of Solomon the King. Translated and edited by S. Liddell MacGregor Mathers. Samuel Weiser, 1989. (Translated and edited from manuscripts on the British Museum. Latin title: *Clavicula Solomonis*.)

Lang, Andrew. *The Grey Fairy Book* (1900).

———. *The Violet Fairy Book* (1901).

Lantiere, Joe. *The Magician's Wand: A History of Mystical Rods of Power*. Revised edition. Olde World Magic, 2004.

LeGuin, Ursula K. *A Wizard of Earthsea*. Bantam Books, 1980.

MacLir, Alferian Gwydion. *Wandlore: The Art of Crafting the Ultimate Magic Tool*. Llewellyn, 2011.

Matheson, P. E., translator. *The Discourses of Epictetus* (1916), www.sacred-texts.com/cla/dep/dep079.htm.

Nigg, Joe. *The Book of Gryphons*. Apple-wood Books, 1982.

Paterson, Jacqueline Memory. *Tree Wisdom: The Definitive Guidebook to the Myth, Folklore, and Healing Power of Trees*. Thorsons, 1996.

Penczak, Christopher. *The Outer Temple of Witchcraft: Circles, Spells, and Rituals*. Llewellyn, 2012.

Pennick, Nigel. *Magical Alphabets: The Secrets and Significance of Ancient Scripts—Including Runes, Greek, Ogham, Hebrew and Alchemical Alphabets*. Red Wheel/Weiser, 1992.

Peterson, Joseph H. "The Magic Wand," http://www.esotericarchives.com/wands/index.html.

Rowling, J. K. *Harry Potter and the Sorcerer's Stone* and sequels. Scholastic Books.

Smith, G. Elliot, "Artemis and the Guardian of the Portal," in *Evolution of the Dragon* (1919), www.sacred-texts.com.

Tolkien, J. R. R. *The Hobbit*. George Allen and Unwin, 1937.

——. *The Lord of the Rings*. George Allen and Unwin, 1965.

Werner, Edward T. C. *Myths and Legends of China* (1922), www.sacred-texts.com. (See chapter XIII, "A Battle of the Gods.")

Zell-Ravenheart, Oberon. *Grimoire for the Apprentice Wizard*. New Page Books, 2004. (See especially the Colors of Magic section.)